Scandalize my

Yusef Komunyakaa is the author of eleven books of poems, including *Neon Vernacular*, *Pleasure Dome* and *Talking Dirty to the Gods*. His collections have won many awards including the Pulitzer and the William Faulkner Prize. In 1999 he was elected a chancellor of the Academy of American Poets. He is a professor in the Council of Humanities and Creative Writing at Princeton University. *Scandalize my Name* is Yusef Komunyakaa's first book-length publication outside the US.

Yusef Komunyakaa

Scandalize my Name

selected poems

PICADOR

This collection first published 2002 by Picador
an imprint of Pan Macmillan Ltd
Pan Macmillan, 20 New Wharf Road, London N1 9RR
Basingstoke and Oxford
Associated companies throughout the world
www.panmacmillan.com

ISBN 0 330 49078 8

Copyright © Yusef Komunyakaa 1979, 1984, 1986, 1988, 1989, 1993, 1998, 2000

All poems from *Talking Dirty to the Gods* © Yusef Komunyakaa 2000
reproduced by permission of Farrar, Straus and Giroux, LLC
All other poems are from *Pleasure Dome: New and Collected Poems* © Yusef Komunyakaa 2001.
Reproduced by permission of Wesleyan University Press. All rights reserved

The right of Yusef Komunyakaa to be identified as the
author of this work has been asserted by him in accordance
with the Copyright, Designs and Patents Act 1988.

All rights reserved. No part of this publication may be
reproduced, stored in or introduced into a retrieval system, or
transmitted, in any form, or by any means (electronic, mechanical,
photocopying, recording or otherwise) without the prior written
permission of the publisher. Any person who does any unauthorized
act in relation to this publication may be liable to criminal
prosecution and civil claims for damages.

9 8 7 6 5 4 3 2 1

A CIP catalogue record for this book is available from
the British Library.

Typeset by SX Composing DTP, Rayleigh, Essex
Printed and bound in Great Britain by
Mackays of Chatham plc, Chatham, Kent

This book is sold subject to the condition that it shall not,
by way of trade or otherwise, be lent, re-sold, hired out,
or otherwise circulated without the publisher's prior consent
in any form of binding or cover other than that in which
it is published and without a similar condition including this
condition being imposed on the subsequent purchaser.

For Reetika and Jehan

Contents

From *Lost in the Bonewheel Factory*

Passions *1*

For You, Sweetheart, I'll Sell Plutonium Reactors *4*

The Nazi Doll *6*

Corrigenda *7*

From *Copacetic*

April Fools' Day *8*

Untitled Blues *10*

Back Then *12*

Blasphemy *13*

Lost Wax *15*

Safe Subjects *17*

Elegy for Thelonious *19*

Copacetic Mingus *21*

Charmed *22*

From *I Apologize for the Eyes in My Head*

Unnatural State of the Unicorn *23*

How I See Things *24*

The Thorn Merchant 26

The Music That Hurts 27

When in Rome – Apologia 28

Audacity of the Lower Gods 30

Dreambook Bestiary 31

Jonestown: More Eyes for *Jadwiga's Dream* 34

The Beast & Burden: Seven Improvisations 35

From ***Dien Cai Dau***

Camouflaging the Chimera 40

Tunnels 42

Starlight Scope Myopia 44

"You and I Are Disappearing" 46

2527th Birthday of the Buddha 47

Re-creating the Scene 48

A Break from the Bush 50

Communiqué 51

The Edge 53

Jungle Surrender 55

Thanks 57

To Have Danced with Death 59

Boat People 60

Bui Doi, Dust of Life 61

Missing in Action 62

Losses 64

Facing It 65

From *February in Sydney*

The Plea 66

Boxing Day 68

Protection of Moveable Cultural Heritage 70

Blue Light Lounge Sutra for the Performance Poets at Harold Park Hotel 71

Venus's-flytraps 73

The Whistle 75

Seasons Between Yes & No 79

The Millpond 81

Immolatus 84

Fleshing-out the Season 86

Blackberries 88

Yellowjackets 89

History Lessons 90

My Father's Love Letters 92

Salomé 94

Slam, Dunk, & Hook 97

From *Neon Vernacular*

Work *98*

Songs for My Father *100*

From *Thieves of Paradise*

Memory Cave *107*

Out There There Be Dragons *109*

The Song Thief *110*

Ode to a Drum *111*

Eclogue at Daybreak *113*

Confluence *114*

Eclogue at Twilight *116*

The Tally *118*

Heroes of Waterloo *120*

In the Mirror *121*

Messages *122*

Bennelong's Blues *123*

Quatrains for Ishi *124*

Nude Interrogation *129*

The Poplars *130*

Surgery *131*

A Summer Night in Hanoi *132*

A Reed Boat *133*

The Hanoi Market *134*

The Deck *135*

Blessing the Animals *136*

The Thorn Merchant's Daughter *138*

The Monkey House *139*

Dolphy's Aviary *141*

Woebegone *142*

Anodyne *143*

From ***Talking Dirty to the Gods***

The Centaur *145*

Ode to the Maggot *146*

Envy *147*

Castrato *148*

Pan *149*

Lust *150*

Happenstance *151*

Gluttony *152*

A Famous Ghost *153*

A Kind of Xenia *154*

Avarice *155*

Rollerblades *156*

Meditations on a File *157*

The God of Land Mines *158*

Postscript to a Summer Night *159*

The God of Variables *160*

Anger *161*

Crow Lingo *162*

Euphony *163*

Passions

Coitus

Ah, pink tip of sixth sense,
oyster fat of lovepearl,
dew-seed & singing leaf-tongue,
lizard's head of pure thought.

Body Painting

To step into the golden lute
& paint one's soul
on the body. Bird
goddess & slow snake
in the flowered tree. Circle,
lineage, womb, mouth, leaf-footed
godanimal on a man's chest
who leaps into the moon
on a woman's belly.

Blue-green Iridescent Flies

Meat, excrement, a source
of life attracts this
message & definition
of the ultimate us.
They fly off
with the weight of the world.

Peepshow

A new moon rises
on an elevator over the mountain.

String Bass

The moon's at the window,
as she rocks in the arms
of this lonely player
like a tall Yoruba woman.

Pinball Machines

Encased in glass, a woman
opens her eyes. The room floods
with a century of bells.
Magnetic balls & sound of metal
seem enough to build a locomotive
moving through the room's wooden bones.

Butterflies

Incandescent anthologies
semi-zoological alphabets of fire,
these short lives transmigrate, topaz
memories cling to air, release wordflesh
from the cocoon of silk fear.

Psilocybe

One hundred purple rooms
in a mirror of black water.
I must enter each,
interrogated by a different demon.
In the distance I can hear
the sea coming. A woman at Laguna Beach.
Her eyes now seashells.
Her arms two far-off sails.
Like a tree drags the ground on a windy day
with yellow & red fruit too soft to eat,
she comes toward me. Stars cluster
her laughter like a nest of moth eyes –
her focus on the world.
The closer she comes, the deeper
I work myself away into music
that I hope can save us both.
A man steps from a junkyard of chrome
fenders & hubcaps,
pulling off masks.
At least a hundred scattered about.
The last one: I am.

For You, Sweetheart,
I'll Sell Plutonium Reactors

For you, sweetheart, I'll ride back down
into black smoke early Sunday morning
cutting fog, grab the moneysack
of gold teeth. Diamond mines
soil creep groan ancient cities, archaeological
diggings, & yellow bulldozers turn around all night
in blood-lit villages. Inhabitants here once gathered
      seashells
that glimmered like pearls. When the smoke clears,
      you'll see
an erected throne like a mountain to scale,
institutions built with bones, guns hidden in walls
that swing open like big-mouthed B-52s.
Your face in the mirror is my face. You tapdance
on tabletops for me, while corporate bosses
arm wrestle in back rooms for your essential downfall.
I entice homosexuals into my basement butcher shop.
I put my hands around another sharecropper's throat
for that mink coat you want from Saks Fifth,
short-change another beggarwoman,
steal another hit song from Sleepy
John Estes, salt another gold mine in Cripple Creek,
drive another motorcycle up a circular ice wall,
face another public gunslinger like a bad chest wound,
just to slide hands under black silk.
Like the Ancient Mariner steering a skeleton ship
against the moon, I'm their hired gunman
if the price is right, take a contract on myself.

They'll name mountains & rivers in my honor.
I'm a drawbridge over manholes for you, sweetheart.
I'm paid two hundred grand
to pick up a red telephone anytime & call up God.
I'm making tobacco pouches out of the breasts of Indian
      maidens
so we can stand in a valley & watch grass grow.

The Nazi Doll

It sits lopsided
in a cage. Membrane.

Vertebra. This precious, white
ceramic doll's brain

twisted out of a knob of tungsten.
It bleeds a crooked smile

& arsenic sizzles in the air.
Its eyes an old lie.

Its bogus tongue, Le Diable.
Its lampshade of memory.

Guilt yahoos, benedictions
in its Cro-Magnon skull

blossom, a flurry of fireflies,
vowels of rattlesnake beads.

Its heart hums the song of dust
like a sweet beehive.

Corrigenda

I take it back.
The crow doesn't have red wings.
They're pages of dust.
The woman in the dark room
takes the barrel of a .357 magnum
out of her mouth, reclines
on your bed, a Helena Rubinstein smile.
I'm sorry, you won't know your father
by his darksome old clothes.
He won't be standing by that tree.
I haven't salted the tail
of the sparrow.
Erase its song from this page.
I haven't seen the moon
fall open at the golden edge of our sleep.
I haven't been there
like the tumor in each of us.
There's no death that can
hold us together like twin brothers
coming home to bury their mother.
I never said there's a book inside
every tree. I never said I know how
the legless beggar feels when
the memory of his toes itch.
If I did, drunkenness
was then my god & naked dancer.
I take it back.
I'm not a suicidal mooncalf;
you don't have to take my shoelaces.
If you must quote me, remember
I said that love heals from inside.

April Fools' Day

They had me laid out in a white
satin casket. What the hell
went wrong, I wanted to ask.
Whose midnight-blue sedan
mowed me down, what unnameable fever
bloomed amber & colchicum
in my brain, which doctor's scalpel
slipped? Did it happen
on a rainy Saturday, blue
Monday, Vallejo's Thursday?
I think I was on a balcony
overlooking the whole thing.
My soul sat in a black chair
near the door, sullen
& no-mouthed. I was fifteen
in a star-riddled box,
in heaven up to my eyelids.
My skin shone like damp light,
my face was the gray of something
gone. They were all there.
My mother behind an opaque veil,
so young. My brothers huddled like stones,
my sister rocked her Shirley Temple
doll to sleep. Three fat ushers fanned
my grandmamas, used smelling salts.
All my best friends – Cowlick,
Sneaky Pete, Happy Jack, Pie Joe,
& Comedown Jones.
I could smell lavender,
a tinge of dust. Their mouths,

palms of their hands
stained with mulberries.
Daddy posed in his navy-blue suit
as doubting Thomas: some twisted
soft need in his eyes, wondering if
I was just another loss
he divided his days into.

Untitled Blues

after a photograph by Yevgeni Yevtushenko

I catch myself trying
to look into the eyes
of the photo, at a black boy
behind a laughing white mask
he's painted on. I
could've been that boy
years ago.
Sure, I could say
everything's copacetic,
listen to a Buddy Bolden cornet
cry from one of those coffin-
shaped houses called
shotgun. We could
meet in Storyville,
famous for quadroons,
with drunks discussing God
around a honky-tonk piano.
We could pretend we can't
see the kitchen help
under a cloud of steam.
Other lurid snow jobs:
night & day, the city
clothed in her see-through
French lace, as pigeons
coo like a beggar chorus
among makeshift studios
on wheels – Vieux Carré
belles having portraits painted

twenty years younger.
We could hand jive
down on Bourbon & Conti
where tap dancers hold
to their last steps,
mammy dolls frozen
in glass cages. The boy
locked inside your camera,
perhaps he's lucky –
he knows how to steal
laughs in a place
where your skin
is your passport.

Back Then

I've eaten handfuls of fire
back to the bright sea
of my first breath
riding the hipbone of memory
& saw a wheel of birds
a bridge into the morning
but that was when gold
didn't burn out a man's eyes
before auction blocks
groaned in courtyards
& nearly got the best of me
that was when the spine
of every ebony tree wasn't
a pale woman's easy chair
black earth-mother of us all
crack in the bones & sombre
eyes embedded like beetles
in stoic heartwood
seldom have I needed
to shake a hornet's nest
from the breastplate
fire over the ground
pain tears me to pieces
at the pottery wheel
of each dawn
an antelope leaps
in the heartbeat
of the talking drum

Blasphemy*

You named those lies clustered
in each rib cage. Attached
to some circular truth, you
glimpsed soldiers of fortune
sweeping their footprints
with branches of mistletoe.
You showed them the corpse garden
couldn't keep blooming,
not forever – black bags
of songs split open at sunrise.
You coped down the earthworm's
calligraphy, broke illusion's hymen,
uncovered the scars smiling
under Dutch silk, translated
the hyena's soliloquy.
You carbon-dated the skull
paperweight on the commissioner's desk
& filled in with charcoal
those mental lapses –
when all the gone ones
resurfaced as dancing rags
in the wind, you named
the beast upon the gallows tree,
its sag-belly dragging
the ground. You appraised

---

* Harold Rubin was tried for blasphemy on the basis of his artwork and exiled from South Africa.

the medieval rot taking hold
of dirt floors, crawling up
the cathedral's high rafters.
Madness, you brought it home.

Lost Wax

I can't help but think
of bodies spoon-fashion
in the belly of a ship.

Gods pour us into the molds
they dream; Legba mends
hope, the breath-cup, footsteps

in plaster of Paris. A bird
so perfect, the wind
steals it from my hand.

Inscription on a vase –
I am whatever it holds,
songs that fit into my mouth.

I am without mercy
because I am what
night poured her lament into,

here on the edge of Kilimanjaro.
All the raw work gone
into each carved ghost

of an antelope, loved
no less than the gods
who spring from our loins.

Woman-mold, man-mold:
whatever shape we think
will save us, what's left

in us preserved by joy.
We won't trade our gods
for money. The hot wax

bubbles up like tar,
& the dream's scaled down
to a gazelle, a figure

with *Benin* printed
on the forehead.
How about a lamp to see by?

Two hands folded together
as a drinking cup,
something that simple.

Safe Subjects

How can love heal
the mouth shut this way?
Say something worth breath.
Let it surface, recapitulate
how fat leeches press down
gently on a sex goddess's eyelids.
Let truth have its way with us
like a fishhook holds
to life, holds dearly to nothing
worth saying – pull it out,
bringing with it hard facts,
knowledge that the fine underbone
of hope is also attached
to inner self, underneath it all.
Undress. No, don't be afraid
even to get Satan mixed up in this
acknowledgement of thorns:
meaning there's madness
in the sperm, in the egg,
fear breathing in its blood sac,
true accounts not so easily
written off the sad book.

Say something about pomegranates.
Say something about real love.
Yes, true love – more than
parted lips, than parted legs
in sorrow's darkroom of potash
& blues. Let the brain stumble
from its hidings place, from its cell block,

to the edge of oblivion
to come to itself, sharp-tongued
as a boar's grin in summer moss
where a vision rides the back
of God, at this masquerade.

Redemptive as a straight razor
against a jugular vein –
unacknowledged & unforgiven.
It's truth we're after here,
hurting for, out in the streets
where my brothers kill each other,
each other's daughters & guardian angels
in the opera of dead on arrival.

Say something that resuscitates
us, behind the masks,
as we stumble off into neon nights
to loveless beds & a second skin
of loneliness. Something political as dust
& earthworms at work in the temple
of greed & mildew, where bowed lamps
cast down shadows like blueprints of graves.
Say something for us who can't believe
in the creed of nightshade.
Yes, say something to us dreamers
who decode the message of dirt
between ancient floorboards
as black widow spiders
lay translucent eggs
in the skull of a dead mole
under a dogwood in full bloom.

Elegy for Thelonious

Damn the snow.
Its senseless beauty
pours a hard light
through the hemlock.
Thelonious is dead. Winter
drifts in the hourglass;
notes pour from the brain cup.
Damn the alley cat
wailing a muted dirge
off Lenox Ave.
Thelonious is dead.
Tonight's a lazy rhapsody of shadows
swaying to blue vertigo
& metaphysical funk.
Black trees in the wind.
Crepuscule with Nelly
plays inside the bowed head.
"Dig the Man Ray of piano!"
O Satisfaction,
hot fingers blur
on those white rib keys.
Coming on the Hudson.
Monk's Dream.
The ghost of bebop
from 52nd Street,
footprints in the snow.
Damn February.
Let's go to Minton's
& play "modern malice"
till daybreak. Lord,

there's Thelonious
wearing that old funky hat
pulled down over his eyes.

Copacetic Mingus

Mingus One, Two and Three.
Which is the image you want the world to see?
– Charles Mingus, *Beneath the Underdog*

Heartstring. Blessed wood
& every moment the thing's made of:
ball of fatback
licked by fingers of fire.
Hard love, it's hard love.
Running big hands down
the upright's wide hips,
rocking his moon-eyed mistress
with gold in her teeth.
Art & life bleed
into each other
as he works the bow.
But tonight we're both a long ways
from the Mile High City,
1973. Here in New Orleans
years below sea level,
I listen to *Pithecanthropus
Erectus*: Up & down, under
& over, every which way –
thump, thump, dada – ah, yes.
Wood heavy with tenderness,
Mingus fingers the loom
gone on Segovia,
dogging the raw strings
unwaxed with rosin.
Hyperbolic bass line. Oh, no!
Hard love, it's hard love.

Charmed

I jump between the cat
& a bird. The cat cries
as though I had struck her with a stick.
If animals possess souls
her cry's close to sin.
She moves toward the bird.
Women have moved gently
toward me – & me toward them –
this way. Some dance
concealed under the skin.
The bird sits perfectly lost
like a flower. So red.
Lost behind the five colors
of the cat's eyes brighter
than truest memory of water.
The cat has pierced him
deeper than bad luck,
moving like a hand buried
in the dark. Years ago
I stepped between a woman & man
at each other's throat,
both turning against me.
I try to shoo the bird away.
I pick him up & his small heart
flutters through me.
The bird has no song left.
I close my eyes,
I place him on the ground,
I back away.

Unnatural State of the Unicorn

Introduce me first as a man.
Don't mention superficial laurels
the dead heap up on the living.
I am a man. Cut me & I bleed.
Before embossed limited editions,
before fat artichoke hearts marinated
in rich sauce & served with imported wines,
before antics & Agnus Dei,
before the stars in your eyes
mean birth sign or Impression,
I am a man. I've scuffled
in mudholes, broken teeth in a grinning skull
like the moon behind bars. I've done it all
to be known as myself. No titles.
I have principles. I won't speak
on the natural state of the unicorn
in literature or self-analysis.
I have no birthright to prove,
no insignia, no secret
password, no fleur-de-lis.
My initials aren't on a branding iron.
I'm standing here in unpolished
shoes & faded jeans, sweating
my manly sweat. Inside my skin,
loving you, I am this space
my body believes in.

How I See Things

I hear you were
sprawled on the cover of *Newsweek*
with freedom marchers, those years
when blood tinted the photographs,
when fire leaped into the trees.

Negatives of nightriders
develop in the brain.
The Strawberry Festival Queen
waves her silk handkerchief,
executing a fancy high kick

flashback through the heart.
Pickups with plastic Jesuses
on dashboards head for hoedowns.
Men run twelve miles into wet cypress
swinging bellropes. Ignis fatuus can't be blamed

for the charred Johnson grass.
Have we earned the right
to forget, forgive
ropes for holding
to moonstruck branches?

Every last stolen whisper
the hoot owl echoes
turns leaves scarlet.
Hush shakes the monkeypod
till pink petal-tongues fall.

You're home in New York.
I'm back here in Bogalusa
with one foot in pinewoods.
The mockingbird's blue note
sounds to me like *please*,

please. A beaten song
threaded through the skull
by cross hairs.
Black hands still turn blood red
working the strawberry fields.

The Thorn Merchant

There are teeth marks
on everything he loves.
When he enters the long room
more solemn than a threadbare Joseph coat,
the Minister of Hard Knocks & Golden Keys
begins to shuffle his feet.
The ink on contracts disappears.
Another stool pigeon leans
over a wrought-iron balcony.
Blood money's at work.
While men in black wetsuits
drag Blue Lake, his hands dally
at the hem of his daughter's skirt.
In the brain's shooting gallery
he goes down real slow.
His heart suspended in a mirror,
shadow of a crow over a lake.
With his fingers around his throat
he moans like a statue
of straw on a hillside.
Ready to auction off his hands
to the highest bidder,
he knows how death waits
in us like a light switch.

The Music That Hurts

Put away those insipid spoons.
The frontal lobe horn section went home hours ago.
The trap drum has been kicked
down the fire escape,
& the tenor's ballad amputated.
Inspiration packed her bags.
Her caftan recurs in the foggy doorway
like brain damage; the soft piano solo of her walk
evaporates; memory loses her exquisite tongue,
looking for "green silk stockings with gold seams"
on a nail over the bathroom mirror.
Tonight I sleep with Silence,
my impossible white wife.

When in Rome – Apologia

Please forgive me, sir
for getting involved

in the music –
it's my innate weakness

for the cello: so human.
Please forgive me
for the attention

I've given your wife
tonight, sir.

I was taken in by her
strands of pearls,
enchanted by a piano
riff in the cortex,
by a secret

anticipation. I don't know
what came over me, sir.

After three Jack Daniel's
you must overlook
my candor, my lack of
sequitur.

I could talk
about Odysseus

& Athena, sexual
flowers, autogamy
or Nothingness.

I got carried away
by the swing of her hips.

But take no offense
if I return to the matter

as if hormonal.
I must confess
my love for black silk, sir.
I apologize for
the eyes in my head.

Audacity of the Lower Gods

I know salt marshes that move along like one big
trembling wing. I've noticed insects
shiny as gold in a blues singer's teeth
& more keenly calibrated than a railroad watch,
but at heart I'm another breed.

The audacity of the lower gods –
whatever we name we own.
Diversiloba, we say, unfolding poison oak.
Lovers go untouched as we lean from bay windows
with telescopes trained on a yellow sky.

I'd rather let the flowers
keep doing what they do best.
Unblessing each petal,
letting go a year's worth of white
death notes, busily unnaming themselves.

Dreambook Bestiary

Fear's Understudy

Like some lost part of a model kit
for Sir Dogma's cracked armor
an armadillo merges with night.
It rests against a mossy stone.
A steel-gray safe-deposit box,
ground level, two quicksilver eyes
peer out from under a coral helmet
color of fossil. It lives
encased in an asbestos hull
at the edge of a kingdom
of blackberries in quagmire,
in a grassy daydream,
sucked into its shield
by logic of flesh.

The Art of Atrophy

The possum plays dead
as Spanish moss, a seasoned actor
giving us his dumb show.
He dreams of ripe persimmons,
watching a dried stick
beside a white thunderstone,
with one eye half-open, a grin
slipping from the crooked corners
of his mouth, that old silver moon
playing tricks again. How long
can he play this waiting game,

till the season collapses,
till blowflies, worms, & ants
crawl into his dull coat
& sneak him away under
the evening star? Now
he's a master escape artist
like Lazarus, the gray
lining from a workman's glove
lost in frost-colored leaves.

Heart of the Rose Garden

A cluster of microscopic mouths
all working at once –

ants improve the soil, sift dust
through a millennium of wings.

They subsist on fear, drawn
to the lovebone,

to the base of the skull
where a slow undermining takes shape.

Under moonlight they begin their
instinctual autopsy, sensing

when grief tracks
someone down in her red patent-leather shoes,

when a man's soul
slips behind a headstone.

Glimpse

Near a spidery cage of grass
this cripple inches sideways up a sandy trail
with its little confiscated burden.
Just bigger than a man's thumbnail,
light as the shadow of a bone.

The sea falls short again. Claws unfold.
Its body almost creeps out. Morning
ticks away. Playing yes, no,
maybe so, it places its dome-shack
down on the sand & backs off,
surveying for the first tremor of loss.

Underside of Light

Centipede. Tubular, bright egg sac
trailing like a lodestone (unable to say
which is dragging which) out of damp compost:
biological soil, miasma, where lightning
starts like a sharp pain in god's spine.

In its armor, this sentinel rises
from a vault of double blackness.
This vegetal love forecasting April
crawls toward murdering light,
first thing tied to last.

Jonestown: More Eyes for *Jadwiga's Dream*

after Rousseau

Brighter than crisp new money.
Birds unfold wings into nervous fans,
adrift like breath-drawn kites, among
tremulous fronds with flowers crimson
as muzzle flash. Tropic silk, root color,
ocean green, they float to tree limbs
like weary scarves.

Hidden eyes deepen the memory
between sunrise & nightmare. Pine-box builders
grin with the pale soothsayer presiding over
this end of songs. The day's a thick hive
of foliage, not the moss grief deposits
on damp stones – we're unable to tell where
fiction bleeds into the real.

Some unspoken voice, small as a lizard's,
is trying to obey the trees.
Green birds flare up behind church bells
against the heartscape: if only
they'd fold their crepe-paper wings
over bruised eyes & see nothing
but night in their brains.

The Beast & Burden: Seven Improvisations

1. The Vicious

Fear threads its song
through the bones.
Syringe, stylus,
or pearl-handled stiletto?
He's fallen in love
with the Spanish garrote;
trailing a blue feather over the beast's belly
on down between his toes.
Night-long laughter
leaks from under the sheet-metal door.
Blackout.

———

He sits under a floodlight
mumbling that a theory of ants
will finally deal with us,

& reading My Lord Rochester
to a golden sky over Johannesburg,
a stray dog beside him, Sirius
licking his combat boots.

2. The Decadent

Herr Scalawag, Esq.
dances the come-on
in Miss Misery's
spike heels.

He does a hellcat
high step stolen
from Josephine Baker,
holding a fake flower
like a flimsy excuse.
A paper rose, poppy
odor of luck
& lust. Look,
he's placed himself
upon the night's maddening wheel,
reduced from flesh
into the stuff
dreams are made of.
                       Hum-job,
his smile working
like a time-released
Mickey Finn.

3. *The Esoteric*

Unable to move the muse with narcotic
sweet talk, he muscles in on someone's grief.

He's on the glassy edge
of his stepping stone, a ghost
puppet stealing light from the real
world. With a wild guess
for spine, a face half-finished
on the blind lithographer's desk.

Canticle, cleftsong & heartriff
stolen out of another's mouth,
effigy's prologue & bravado.
He fingers his heirloom

Bible with rows of exed out names
& dried roses between yellow pages,

searching for an idiom
based on the color of his eyes.

4. *The Sanctimonious*

She wakes to find herself washing
the beast's wounds.
The Woman at the Well
with bare feet in compost,
emissary to the broken. She leans

her body against this born loser,
her hip into his ungodly mercy,
her hair sways with his breathing,
her mind intent on an hourglass
on a stone shelf. Bronze green.

By now, as they rock
in each other's embrace
in the cold half-light,
she knows every doubtful wish
inside his housebroken head.

5. *The Vindictive*

Smiley, the jailer
hums the bowstring's litany.
His pale voice breaks
into a bittersweetness,
his face no more
than a half-page

profile from a wanted poster.
The iron door eases open.
Blameful mask, memory's
notorious white glove
unstitches the heartstring.
His leaden stare tabulates
the spinal column like a throw
of the dice. Satisfied
defeat has taken root,
he smiles down at the prisoner
on the cell floor, his touch
burning like candlelight & crab lice
through black hair. Wagner's
Ring of the Nibelung
plays on radio across the corridor
& the smell of mignonette
comes through the bars. He
tightens his mystical sleephold –
a carbuncle of joy
underneath his kiss.

6. *Exorcism*

The beast's charisma
unravels the way a smoke flower
turns into dust. Hugging
the shadow of a broken wing
beauty & ugliness conspire.
Forced to use his weight perfectly
against himself, the beast is
transmogrified into the burden
& locked in wooden stocks
braced by a cross to bear.

O how geranium-scented melancholia
works on the body –
smell of ether, gut string
trailing lost memories.
Detached form whatever remains,
one note of bliss still burns his tongue.

7. *Epilogue: Communion*

The beast & the burden lock-step waltz. Tiger lily & screwworm, it all adds up to this: bloodstar & molecular burning kiss. Conception. The grooved sockets slip into each other, sinking into pain, a little deeper into earth's habit. Tongue in juice meat, uncertain conversion, cock & heart entangled, ragweed in bloom. A single sigh of glory, the two put an armlock on each other – matched for strength, leg over leg. Double bind & slow dance on ball-bearing feet. Arm in arm & slipknot. Birth, death, back to back – silent mouth against the other's ear. They sing a duet: e pluribus unum. The spirit hinged to a single tree. No deeper color stolen from midnight sky – they're in the same shape, as meat collects around a bone, almost immortal, like a centaur's future perfect dream.

Camouflaging the Chimera

We tied branches to our helmets.
We painted our faces & rifles
with mud from a riverbank,

blades of grass hung from the pockets
of our tiger suits. We wove
ourselves into the terrain,
content to be a hummingbird's target.

We hugged bamboo & leaned
against a breeze off the river,
slow-dragging with ghosts

from Saigon to Bangkok,
with women left in doorways
reaching in from America.
We aimed at dark-hearted songbirds.

In our way station of shadows
rock apes tried to blow our cover,
throwing stones at the sunset. Chameleons

crawled our spines, changing from day
to night: green to gold,
gold to black. But we waited
till the moon touched metal,

till something almost broke
inside us. VC struggled
with the hillside, like black silk

wrestling iron through grass.
We weren't there. The river ran
through our bones. Small animals took refuge
against our bodies; we held our breath,

ready to spring the L-shaped
ambush, as a world revolved
under each man's eyelid.

Tunnels

Crawling down headfirst into the hole,
he kicks the air & disappears.
I feel like I'm down there
with him, moving ahead, pushed
by a river of darkness, feeling
blessed for each inch of the unknown.
Our tunnel rat is the smallest man
in the platoon, in an echo chamber
that makes his ears bleed
when he pulls the trigger.
He moves as if trying to outdo
blind fish easing toward imagined blue,
pulled by something greater than life's
ambitions. He can't think about
spiders & scorpions mending the air,
or care about bats upside down
like gods in the mole's blackness.
The damp smell goes deeper
than the stench of honey buckets.
A web of booby traps waits, ready
to spring into broken stars.
Forced onward by some need,
some urge, he knows the pulse
of mysteries & diversions
like thoughts trapped in the ground.
He questions each root.
Every cornered shadow has a life
to bargain with. Like an angel
pushed against what hurts,
his globe-shaped helmet

follows the gold ring his flashlight
casts into the void. Through silver
lice, shit, maggots, & vapour of pestilence,
he goes, the good soldier,
on hands & knees, tunneling past
death sacked into a blind corner,
loving the weight of the shotgun
that will someday dig his grave.

Starlight Scope Myopia

Gray-blue shadows lift
shadows onto an oxcart.

Making night work for us,
the starlight scope brings
men into killing range.

The river under Vi Bridge
takes the heart away

like the Water God
riding his dragon.
Smoke-colored

Viet Cong
move under our eyelids,

lords over loneliness
winding like coral vine through
sandalwood & lotus,

inside our lowered heads
years after this scene

ends. The brain closes
down. What looks like
one step into the trees,

they're lifting crates of ammo
& sacks of rice, swaying

under their shared weight.
Caught in the infrared,
what are they saying?

Are they talking about women
or calling the Americans

beaucoup dien cai dau?
One of them is laughing.
You want to place a finger

to his lips & say "shhhh."
You try reading ghost talk

on their lips. They say
"up-up we go," lifting as one.
This one, old, bowlegged,

you feel you could reach out
& take him into your arms. You

peer down the sights of your M-16,
seeing the full moon
loaded on an oxcart.

"You and I Are Disappearing"

– Björn Håkansson

The cry I bring down from the hills
belongs to a girl still burning
inside my head. At daybreak
        she burns like a piece of paper.
She burns like foxfire
in a thigh-shaped valley.
A skirt of flames
dances around her
at dusk.
        We stand with our hands
hanging at our sides,
while she burns
        like a sack of dry ice.
She burns like oil on water.
She burns like a cattail torch
dipped in gasoline.
She glows like the fat tip
of a banker's cigar,
        silent as quicksilver.
A tiger under a rainbow
   at nightfall.
She burns like a shot glass of vodka.
She burns like a field of poppies
at the edge of a rain forest.
She rises like dragonsmoke
   to my nostrils.
She burns like a burning bush
driven by a godawful wind.

2527th Birthday of the Buddha

When the motorcade rolled to a halt, Quang Duc
climbed out & sat down in the street.
He crossed his legs,
& the other monks & nuns grew around him like petals.
He challenged the morning sun,
debating with the air
he leafed through – visions brought down to earth.
Could his eyes burn the devil out of men?
A breath of peppermint oil
soothed someone's cry. Beyond terror made flesh –
he burned like a bundle of black joss sticks.
A high wind that started in California
fanned flames, turned each blue page,
leaving only his heart intact.
Waves of saffron robes bowed to the gasoline can.

Re-creating the Scene

The metal door groans
& folds shut like an ancient turtle
that won't let go
of a finger till it thunders.
The Confederate flag
flaps from a radio antenna,
& the woman's clothes
come apart in their hands.
Their mouths find hers
in the titanic darkness
of the steel grotto,
as she counts the names of dead
ancestors, shielding a baby
in her arms. The three men
ride her breath, grunting
over lovers back in Mississippi.
She floats on their rage
like a torn water flower,
defining night inside a machine
where men are gods.
The season quietly sweats.
They hold her down
with their eyes,
taking turns, piling stones
on her father's grave.

The APC rolls with curves of the land,
up hills & down into gullies,
crushing trees & grass,
droning like a constellation

of locusts eating through bamboo,
creating the motion for their bodies.

She rises from the dust
& pulls the torn garment
around her, staring after the APC
till it's small enough
to fit like a toy tank in her hands.
She turns in a circle,
pounding the samarium dust
with her feet where the steel
tracks have plowed. The sun
fizzes like a pill in a glass
of water, & for a moment
the world's future tense:
She approaches the MPs
at the gate; a captain from G-5
accosts her with candy kisses;
I inform *The Overseas Weekly*;
flashbulbs refract her face
in a room of polished brass
& spit-shined boots;
on the trial's second day
she turns into mist –
someone says money
changed hands,
& someone else swears
she's buried at LZ Gator.
But for now, the baby
makes a fist & grabs at the air,
searching for a breast.

A Break from the Bush

The South China Sea
drives in another herd.
The volleyball's a punching bag:
Clem's already lost a tooth
& Johnny's left eye is swollen shut.
Frozen airlifted steaks burn
on a wire grill, & miles away
machine guns can be heard.
Pretending we're somewhere else,
we play harder.
Lee Otis, the point man,
high on Buddha grass,
buries himself up to his neck
in sand. "Can you see me now?
In this spot they gonna build
a Hilton. Invest in Paradise.
Bang, bozos! You're dead."
Frenchie's cassette player
unravels Hendrix's "Purple Haze."
Snake, 17, from Daytona,
sits at the water's edge,
the ash on his cigarette
pointing to the ground
like a crooked finger. CJ,
who in three days will trip
a fragmentation mine,
runs after the ball
into the whitecaps,
laughing.

Communiqué

Bob Hope's on stage, but we want the Gold Diggers,
want a flash of legs

through the hemorrhage of vermilion, giving us
something to kill for.

We want our hearts wrung out like rags & ground down
to Georgia dust

while Cobras drag the perimeter, gliding along the sea,
swinging searchlights

through the trees. The assault & battery of hot pink
glitter erupts

as the rock 'n' roll band tears down the night – caught
in a safety net

of brightness, The Gold Diggers convulse. White legs
shimmer like strobes.

The lead guitarist's right foot's welded to his wah-wah.
"I thought you said

Aretha was gonna be here." "Man, I don't wanna see
no Miss America."

"There's Lola." The sky is blurred by magnesium flares
over the fishing boats.

"Shit, man, she looks awful white to me." We duck
when we hear the quick

metallic hiss of the mountain of amplifiers struck by
a flash of rain.

After the show's packed up & gone, after the choppers have flown out backwards,

after the music & colors have died slowly in our heads, & the downpour's picked up,

we sit holding our helmets like rain-polished skulls.

The Edge

When guns fall silent for an hour
or two, you can hear the cries

of women making love to soldiers.
They have an unmerciful memory

& know how to wear bright dresses
to draw a crowd, conversing

with a platoon of shadows
numbed by morphine. Their real feelings

make them break like April
into red blossoms.

Cursing themselves in ragged dreams
fire has singed the edges of,

they know a slow dying the fields have come
       to terms with.
Shimmering fans work against the heat

& smell of gunpowder, making money
float from hand to hand. The next moment

a rocket pushes a white fist
through night sky, & they scatter like birds

& fall into the shape their lives
have become.

"You want a girl, GI?"
"You buy me Saigon tea?"

Soldiers bring the scent of burning flesh
with them – on their clothes & in their hair,

drawn to faces in half-lit rooms.
As good-bye kisses are thrown

to the charred air, silhouettes of jets
ease over nude bodies on straw mats.

Jungle Surrender

after Don Cooper's painting

Ghosts share us with the past & future
but we struggle to hold on to each breath.

Moving toward what waits behind the trees,
the prisoner goes deeper into himself, away

from how a man's heart divides him, deeper
into the jungle's indigo mystery & beauty,

with both hands raised into the air, only
surrendering halfway: the small man inside

waits like a photo in a shirt pocket, refusing
to raise his hands, silent & uncompromising

as the black scout dog beside him. Love & hate
flesh out the real man, how he wrestles

himself through a hallucination of blues
& deep purples that set the day on fire.

He sleepwalks a labyrinth of violet,
measuring footsteps from one tree to the next,

knowing we're all somehow connected.
What would I have said?

The real interrogator is a voice within.
I would have told them about my daughter

in Phoenix, how young she was,
about my first woman, anything

but how I helped ambush two Viet Cong
while I plugged into the Grateful Dead.

For some, a soft windy voice makes them
snap. Blues & purples. Some place between

central Georgia & Tay Ninh Province –
the vision of a knot of blood unravels

& parts of us we dared put into the picture
come together; the prisoner goes away

almost whole. But he will always touch
fraying edges of things, to feel hope break

like the worm that rejoins itself
under the soil . . . head to tail.

Thanks

Thanks for the tree
between me & a sniper's bullet.
I don't know what made the grass
sway seconds before the Viet Cong
raised his soundless rifle.
Some voice always followed,
telling me which foot
to put down first.
Thanks for deflecting the ricochet
against that anarchy of dusk.
I was back in San Francisco
wrapped up in a woman's wild colors,
causing some dark bird's love call
to be shattered by daylight
when my hands reached up
& pulled a branch away
from my face. Thanks
for the vague white flower
that pointed to the gleaming metal
reflecting how it is to be broken
like mist over the grass,
as we played some deadly
game for blind gods.
What made me spot the monarch
writhing on a single thread
tied to a farmer's gate,
holding the day together
like an unfingered guitar string,
is beyond me. Maybe the hills
grew weary & leaned a little in the heat.

Again, thanks for the dud
hand grenade tossed at my feet
outside Chu Lai. I'm still
falling through its silence.
I don't know why the intrepid
sun touched the bayonet,
but I know that something
stood among those lost trees
& moved only when I moved.

To Have Danced with Death

The black sergeant first class
who stalled us on the ramp
didn't kiss the ground either.

When two hearses sheened up to the plane
& government silver-gray coffins
rolled out on silent chrome coasters,

did he feel better? The empty left leg
of his trousers shivered as another hearse
with shiny hubcaps rolled from behind a building . . .

his three rows of ribbons rainbowed
over the forest of faces through
plate glass. Afternoon sunlight

made surgical knives out of chrome
& brass. He half smiled when
the double doors opened for him

a wordless mouth taking back promises.
The room of blue eyes averted his.
He stood there, searching

his pockets for something:
maybe a woman's name & number
worn thin as a Chinese fortune.

I wanted him to walk ahead,
to disappear through glass,
to be consumed by music

that might move him like Sandman Sims,
but he merely rocked on his good leg
like a bleak & soundless bell.

Boat People

After midnight they load up.
A hundred shadows move about blindly.
Something close to sleep
hides low voices drifting
toward a red horizon. Tonight's
a black string, the moon's pull –
this boat's headed somewhere.
Lucky to have gotten past
searchlights low-crawling the sea,
like a woman shaking water
from her long dark hair.

Twelve times in three days
they've been lucky,
clinging to each other in gray mist.
Now Thai fishermen gaze out across
the sea as it changes color,
hands shading their eyes
the way sailors do,
minds on robbery & rape.
Sunlight burns blood-orange.

Storm warnings crackle on a radio.
The Thai fishermen turn away.
Not enough water for the trip.
The boat people cling to each other,
faces like yellow sea grapes,
wounded by doubt & salt.
Dusk hangs over the water.
Seasick, they daydream Jade Mountain
a whole world away, half-drunk
on what they hunger to become.

Bui Doi, Dust of Life

You drifted from across the sea
under a carmine moon,
framed now in my doorway
by what I tried to forget.
Curly-headed & dark-skinned,
you couldn't escape
eyes taking you apart.
Come here, son, let's see
if they castrated you.

Those nights I held your mother
against me like a half-broken
shield. The wind's refrain
etched my smile into your face –
is that how you found me?
You were born disappearing.
You followed me, blameless
as a blackbird in Hue
singing from gutted jade.

Son, you were born with dust
on your eyelids, but you bloomed up
in a trench where stones were
stacked to hold you down.
With only your mother's name,
you've inherited the inchworm's
foot of earth. *Bui doi*.
I blow the dust off my hands
but it flies back in my face.

Missing in Action

Men start digging in the ground,
propping shadows against trees
outside Hanoi, but there aren't
enough bones for a hash pipe.
After they carve new names
into polished black stone,
we throw dust to the wind
& turn faces to blank walls.

Names we sing in sleep & anger
cling to willows like river mist.
We splice voices on tapes
but we can't make one man
walk the earth again.
Not a single song comes alive
in the ring of broken teeth
on the ground. Sunlight
presses down for an answer.
But nothing can make that C-130
over Hanoi come out of its spin,
spiraling like a flare in green sky.

After the flag's folded,
the living fall
into each other's arms.
They've left spaces
trees can't completely fill.
Pumping breath down tunnels
won't help us bring ghosts
across the sea.

Peasants outside Pakse City
insist the wildflowers
have changed colors.
They're what the wind
& rain have taken back,
what love couldn't recapture.
Now less than a silhouette
grown into the parrot perch,
this one died looking up at the sky.

Losses

After Nam he lost himself,
    not trusting his hands
        with loved ones.

His girlfriend left,
    & now he scouts the edge of town,
        always with one ear

cocked & ready to retreat,
    to blend with hills, poised
        like a slipknot

becoming a noose.
    Unlike punji stakes,
        his traps only snag the heart.

Sometimes he turns in a circle
    until a few faces from Dak To
        track him down.

A dress or scarf in the distance
    can nail him to a dogwood.
        Down below, to his left,

from where the smog rises,
    a small voice reaches his ear
        somehow. No, never mind –

he's halfway back, closer to a ravine,
    going deeper into saw vines,
        in behind White Cove,

following his mind like a dark lover,
    away from car horns & backfire
        where only days are stolen.

Facing It

My black face fades,
hiding inside the black granite.
I said I wouldn't
dammit: No tears.
I'm stone. I'm flesh.
My clouded reflection eyes me
like a bird of prey, the profile of night
slanted against morning. I turn
this way – the stone lets me go.
I turn that way – I'm inside
the Vietnam Veterans Memorial
again, depending on the light
to make a difference.
I go down the 58,022 names,
half-expecting to find
my own in letters like smoke.
I touch the name Andrew Johnson;
I see the booby trap's white flash.
Names shimmer on a woman's blouse
but when she walks away
the names stay on the wall.
Brushstrokes flash, a red bird's
wings cutting across my stare.
The sky. A plane in the sky.
A white vet's image floats
closer to me, then his pale eyes
look through mine. I'm a window.
He's lost his right arm
inside the stone. In the black mirror
a woman's trying to erase names:
No, she's brushing a boy's hair.

The Plea

Round about midnight
    the clock's ugly stare
hangs in mental repose
    & its antimagnetic second hand
measures a man's descent.
    The bottom falls out
of each dream – the silver spike
    in my hands & I'm on the floor.
The Alice in Malice
    does a little soft shoe
on my troubled heart.
    Hot & heavy,
cool & cosmic honeydripper
    fingers play the missing notes
inbetween life & death
    round midnight. Lost
lovers in my empty doorway
    groove to a sweet pain
in the bruise-colored neon
    where my soul weaves
itself into *terra incognita*,
    into the blue & green
sounds of Botany Bay
    reflected like rozellas
through the big, black
    slow dance of waves grinding
against the shore. Thelonious
    & bright as that golden plea
of gospel under everything
    Monk wrung from the keys.

Round about midnight
    despair returns each minute
like a drop of moonshine
    elongating into rapture
moaned through Bird's mouthpiece
    in a soundproof room
where trust & love
    is white dust on the dark
furniture. Time is nothing
    but an endless bridge.
All those who thought
    they could use my body
for nowhere's roadmap
    I see their blank faces
float up from the whirlpool
    as the turntable spins.
Each undying note resounds.
    There's a cry in every pocket
& low swell of unhappy
    lust I've suffered,
& round about midnight the odor of sex
    & salvation quivers in each song
the wooden hammers
    strike from wire strings
like anger stolen back
    from the soil.

Boxing Day

Burns never landed a blow.
It was hopeless, preposterous, heroic.
– Jack London

This is where Jack Johnson
cornered Tommy Burns in 1908.
Strong as an ironbark
tree, he stood there
flexing his biceps
till he freed
the prisoner under his skin.
    The bell clanged
    & a profusion of voices
    shook the afternoon. Johnson
    jabbed with the power
    of an engine throwing a rod,
    & Burns sleepwalked
    to the spinning edge
of the planet like a moth
drawn to a burning candle.
He was dizzy as a drunken girl
tangoing with a flame tree
breaking into full bloom,
burdened by fruits of desire
& the smell of carnival.
    A currawong crossed the sun
    singing an old woman's cry.
    The referee threw in his towel
    in the fourteenth round & bookies
    scribbled numbers beside names

      madly, as twenty thousand rose
      into the air like a wave.
For years the razor-gang boys
bragged about how they would've KOed
Johnson, dancing & punching each day.
Eighty years later, the stadium's
checkered with tennis courts,
a plantation of pale suits
called White City.
      I hear Miles Davis' trumpet
      & Leadbelly's "Titanic."
      A bell's metal treble
      reverberates . . . the sunset
      moves like a tremble of muscle
      across Rushcutters Bay,
      back to the name Johnson
flashing over the teletype
when he danced The Eagle Rock,
drove fast cars & had a woman
on each arm, to Jesse Willard
pushing him down into a whirlpool's
death roll under white
confetti & cheers in Havana.

Protection of Moveable Cultural Heritage

Time-polished skulls of Yagan & Pemulwy
sit in a glass cage wired to a burglar alarm
in Britain, but the jaws of these two
resistance leaders haven't been broken
into a lasting grin for the empire.

Under fluorescent lamps they're crystal balls
into which one can gaze & see the past.
With eyes reflected into empty sockets
through the glass, I can't stop reading
an upside-down newspaper

headlining Klaus Barbie, Karl Linnas
& Bernhard Goetz. The skulls sit
like wax molds for Fear & Anger –
beheaded body-songs lament & recall
how windy grass once sang to the feet.

Now, staring from their display case,
they still govern a few broken hearts
wandering across the Nullarbor Plain.
Killed fighting for love of birthplace
under a sky ablaze with flying foxes

& shiny crows, they remember the weight
of chains inherited from the fathers
of bushrangers, how hatred runs into
the soul like red veins in the eye
or thin copper threads through money.

Blue Light Lounge Sutra for the Performance Poets at Harold Park Hotel

the need gotta be
so deep words can't
answer simple questions
all night long notes
stumble off the tongue
& color the air indigo
so deep fragments of gut
& flesh cling to the song
you gotta get into it
so deep salt crystallizes on eyelashes
the need gotta be
so deep you can vomit up ghosts
& not feel broken
till you are no more
than a half ounce of gold
in painful brightness
you gotta get into it
blow that saxophone
so deep all the sex & dope in this world
can't erase your need
to howl against the sky
the need gotta be
so deep you can't
just wiggle your hips
& rise up out of it
chaos in the cosmos
modern man in the pepperpot
you gotta get hooked

into every hungry groove
so deep the bomb locked
in rust opens like a fist
into it into it so deep
rhythm is pre-memory
the need gotta be basic
animal need to see
& know the terror
we are made of honey
cause if you wanna dance
this boogie be ready
to let the devil use your head
for a drum.

Venus's-flytraps

I am five,
    Wading out into deep
        Sunny grass,
Unmindful of snakes
    & yellowjackets, out
        To the yellow flowers
Quivering in sluggish heat.
    Don't mess with me
        'Cause I have my Lone Ranger
Six-shooter. I can't hurt
    You with questions
        Like silver bullets.
The tall flowers in my dreams are
    Big as the First State Bank,
        & they eat all the people
Except the ones I love.
    They have women's names,
        With mouths like where
Babies come from. I am five.
    I'll dance for you
        If you close your eyes. No
Peeping through your fingers.
    I don't supposed to be
        This close to the tracks.
One afternoon I saw
    What a train did to a cow.
        Sometimes I stand so close
I can see the eyes
    Of men hiding in boxcars.
        Sometimes they wave

    & holler for me to get back. I laugh
        When trains make the dogs
            Howl. Their ears hurt.
I also know bees
    Can't live without flowers.
        I wonder why Daddy
Calls Mama honey.
    All the bees in the world
        Live in little white houses
Except the ones in these flowers.
    All sticky & sweet inside.
        I wonder what death tastes like.
Sometimes I toss the butterflies
    Back into the air.
        I wish I knew why
The music in my head
    Makes me scared.
        But I know things
I don't supposed to know.
    I could start walking
        & never stop.
These yellow flowers
    Go on forever.
        Almost to Detroit.
Almost to the sea.
    My mama says I'm a mistake.
        That I made her a bad girl.
My playhouse is underneath
    Our house, & I hear people
        Telling each other secrets.

The Whistle

1

The seven o'clock whistle
Made the morning air fulvous
With a metallic syncopation,
A key to a door in the sky – opening
& closing flesh. The melody
Men & women built lives around,
Sonorous as the queen bee's fat
Hum drawing workers from flowers,
Back to the colonized heart.
A titanous puff of steam rose
From the dragon trapped below
Iron, bricks & wood.
The whole black machine
Shuddered, blue jays & redbirds
Wove light through leaves
& something dead under the foundation
Brought worms to life.
Men capped their thermoses,
Switched off Loretta Lynn,
& slid from trucks & cars.
The rip saws throttled
& swung out over logs
On conveyor belts.
Daddy lifted the tongs
To his right shoulder . . . a winch
Uncoiled the steel cable
From its oily scrotum;
He waved to the winchman

& iron teeth bit into pine.
Yellow forklifts darted
With lumber to boxcars
Marked for distant cities.
At noon, Daddy would walk
Across the field of goldenrod
& mustard weed, the pollen
Bright & sullen on his overalls.
He'd eat on our screened-in
Back porch – red beans & rice
With ham hocks & cornbread.
Lemonade & peach jello.

The one o'clock bleat
Burned sweat & salt into afternoon
& the wheels within wheels
Unlocked again, pulling rough boards
Into the plane's pneumatic grip.
Wild geese moved like a wedge
Between sky & sagebrush,
As Daddy pulled the cable
To the edge of the millpond
& sleepwalked cypress logs.
The day turned on its axle
& pyramids of russet sawdust
Formed under corrugated
Blowpipes fifty feet high.
The five o'clock whistle
Bellowed like a bull, controlling
Clocks on kitchen walls;
Women dabbed loud perfume
Behind their ears & set tables
Covered with flowered oilcloth.

2

When my father was kicked by the foreman,
He booted him back,
& his dreams slouched into an aftershock
Of dark women whispering
To each other. Like petals of a black rose
In one of Busby Berkeley's
Oscillating dances in a broken room. Shadows,
Runagates & Marys.
The steel-gray evening was a canvas
Zigzagged with questions
Curling up from smokestacks, as dusky birds
Brushed blues into a montage
Traced back to *L'Amistad* & the psychosis
Behind *Birth of a Nation*.
With eyes against glass & ears to diaphanous doors,
I heard a cornered prayer.
Car lights rubbed against our windows,
Ravenous as snow wolves.
A brick fell into the livingroom like a black body,
& a riot of drunk curses
Left the gladioli & zinnias
Maimed. Double dares
Took root in night soil.
The whistle boiled
Gutbucket underneath silence
& burned with wrath.
But by then Daddy was with Uncle James
Outside The Crossroad,
Their calloused fingers caressing the .38
On the seat of the pickup;
Maybe it was the pine-scented moonglow

That made him look so young
& faceless, wearing his mother's powder blue
Sunday dress & veiled hat.

Seasons Between Yes & No

1

We stood so the day slanted
Through our dime-store magnifying glass.
Girls laughed & swayed, caught
On the wild edge of our scent.
A scorpion of sunlight crawled
Each boy's arm, as we took turns
Daring each other to flinch. Not
Knowing what a girl's smile did,
An oath stitched us to God.

2

Ice & wind cut through trees
Quick as Pompeian lava casting lovers
Into the arms of strange gods.
We brought in two robins,
& the heat from our hands made them fly
A few clumsy feet.
But half-drugged, rising out of hypnosis,
They broke their bodies
Against breath-fogged panes.

3

We held back curses,
Torturing each other with an adagio
Of silence. Little Faust
Games of the heart.
Bets. Dares. Sucker bait.
Romantic & obscene,
We held back cries,
Letting the mosquitoes suck
Till they popped like stars of blood through cloth.

The Millpond

They looked like wood ibis
From a distance, & as I got closer
They became knots left for gods
To undo, like bows tied
At the center of weakness.
Shadow to light, mind to flesh,
Swamp orchids quivered under green hats,
Nudged by slate-blue catfish
Headed for some boy's hook
On the other side. The day's
Uncut garments of fallen chances
Stumbled among flowers
That loved only darkness,
As afternoon came through underbrush
Like a string of firecrackers
Tied to a dog's tail.
Gods lived under that mud
When I was young & sublimely
Blind. Each bloom a shudder
Of uneasiness, no sound
Except the whippoorwill.
They conspired to become twilight
& metaphysics, as five-eyed
Fish with milky bones
Flip-flopped in oily grass.

*

We sat there as the moon rose
Up from chemical water,
Phosphorous as an orange lantern.

An old man shifted
His three-pronged gig
Like a New Guinea spear,
So it could fly quicker
Than a frog's tongue or angry word.
He pointed to snapping turtles
Posed on cypress logs,
armored in stillness,
Slow kings of a dark world.
We knelt among cattails.
The reflection of a smokestack
Cut the black water in half.
A circle of dry leaves
Smouldered on the ground
For mosquitoes. As if
To draw us to them, like decoys
For some greater bounty,
The choir of bullfrogs called,
Singing a cruel happiness.

*

Sometimes I'd watch them
Scoot back into their tunnels,
Down in a gully where
The pond's overflow drained . . .
Where shrub oak & banyan
Grew around barbed wire
Till April oozed sap
Like a boy beside a girl
Squeezing honeycomb in his fists.
I wondered if time tied
Everything to goldenrod
Reaching out of cow manure for the sun.
What did it have to do

With saw & hammer,
With what my father taught me
About this world? Sometimes
I sat reading *Catcher in the Rye*,
& other times *Spider Man*
& *Captain Marvel*. Always
After a rain crawfish surfaced
To grab the salt meat
Tied to the nylon string,
Never knowing when they left
The water & hit the bottom
Of my tincan. They clung
To desire, like the times
I clutched something dangerous
& couldn't let go.

Immolatus

She had her feet in the trough,
Nosing into the golden corn,
When daddy did a half spin
& brought down the sledgehammer.
She sank to the mud.
An oak branch bowed
As they tightened the rope
To a creaky song of pulley wheels.
A few leaves left
For the wind to whip down,
They splashed hot water
& shaved her with blades
That weighed less each year.
Snow geese honked overhead
& Sirius balanced on a knifetip.
Wintertime bit into the ropy guts
Falling into a number-3 tub
That emptied out in a gray gush
Like the end of a ditch
Choked with slime & roses.
Something love couldn't make
Walk again. I had a boy's job
Lugging water from the pump
& filling the iron washpot.
I threw pine knots on the blaze.
Soon her naked whiteness
Was a silence to split
Between helpers & owner.
Liver, heart, & head
Flung to a foot tub.

They smiled as she passed
Through their hands. Next day
I tracked blood in a circle
Across dead grass, while fat
Boiled down to lye soap.

Fleshing-out the Season

They said he lived in both houses.
That the black woman
Once worked as a maid
For his wife. The women
Sometimes met in town & talked
Like old friends, would hug & kiss
Before parting. They said
The man's father was a big-time
Politician in Jackson, Mississippi,
& owned a cotton gin,
& the Klan didn't dare hassle
Him. The black woman's house
Was a scaled-down replica
Of the other: both yards
A jungle of bougainvillea,
Azalea, & birds of paradise.
They said there's a picture
Of the three at Mardi Gras
Dancing in a circle of flambeaus.
In summer he always ate
Cones of raspberry ice cream,
& carried a fat ledger
From house to house. Alyce
Clover grew over his pathway.
He sent his white son to Vanderbilt,
The black one to Columbia.
He had read Blake aloud to them;
Pointed out Orion & Venus.
They said both women waited
To divide him. One sprinkled him

Over the Gulf of Mexico,
& the other put him under roots
Of pigweed beside the back gate—
Purple, amaranthine petals,
She wore in her hair on Sundays.

Blackberries

They left my hands like a printer's
Or thief's before a police blotter
& pulled me into early morning's
Terrestrial sweetness, so thick
The damp ground was consecrated
Where they fell among a garland of thorns.

Although I could smell old lime-covered
History, at ten I'd still hold out my hands
& berries fell into them. Eating from one
& filling a half gallon with the other,
I ate the mythology & dreamt
Of pies & cobbler, almost

Needful as forgiveness. My bird dog Spot
Eyed blue jays & thrashers. The mud frogs
In rich blackness, hid from daylight.
An hour later, beside City Limits Road
I balanced a gleaming can in each hand,
Limboed between worlds, repeating *one dollar*.

The big blue car made me sweat.
Wintertime crawled out of the windows.
When I leaned closer I saw the boy
& girl my age, in the wide back seat
Smirking, & it was then I remembered my fingers
Burning with thorns among berries too ripe to touch.

Yellowjackets

When the plowblade struck
An old stump hiding under
The soil like a beggar's
Rotten tooth, they swarmed up
& Mister Jackson left the plow
Wedged like a whaler's harpoon.
The horse was midnight
Against dusk, tethered to somebody's
Pocketwatch. He shivered, but not
The way women shook their heads
Before mirrors at the five
& dime – a deeper connection
To the low field's evening star.
He stood there, in tracechains,
Lathered in froth, just
Stopped by a great, goofy
Calmness. He whinnied
Once, & then the whole
Beautiful, blue-black sky
Fell on his back.

History Lessons

1

Squinting up at leafy sunlight, I stepped back
& shaded my eyes, but couldn't see what she pointed to.
The courthouse lawn where the lone poplar stood
Was almost flat as a pool table. Twenty-five
Years earlier it had been a stage for half the town:
Cain & poor whites at a picnic on saint augustine
Grass. No, I couldn't see the piece of blonde rope.
I stepped closer to her, to where we were almost
In each other's arms, & then spotted the flayed
Tassel of wind-whipped hemp knotted around a limb
Like a hank of hair, a weather-whitened bloom
In hungry light. That was where they prodded him
Up into the flatbed of a pickup.

2

We had coffee & chicory with lots of milk,
Hoecakes, bacon, & gooseberry jam. She told me
How a white woman in The Terrace
Said that she shot a man who tried to rape her,
How their car lights crawled sage fields
Midnight to daybreak, how a young black boxer
Was running & punching the air at sunrise,
How they tarred & feathered him & dragged the corpse
Behind a Model T through the Mill Quarters,
How they dumped the prizefighter on his
      mother's doorstep,
How two days later three boys

Found a white man dead under the trestle
In blackface, the woman's bullet
In his chest, his head on a clump of sedge.

3

When I stepped out on the back porch
The pick-up man from Bogalusa Dry Cleaners
Leaned against his van, with an armload
Of her Sunday dresses, telling her
Emmett Till had begged for it
With his damn wolf whistle.
She was looking at the lye-scoured floor,
White as his face. The hot words
Swarmed out of my mouth like African bees
& my fists were cocked,
Hammers in the air. He popped
The clutch when he turned the corner,
As she pulled me into her arms
& whispered, *Son, you ain't gonna live long.*

My Father's Love Letters

On Fridays he'd open a can of Jax
After coming home from the mill,
& ask me to write a letter to my mother
Who sent postcards of desert flowers
Taller than men. He would beg,
Promising to never beat her
Again. Somehow I was happy
She had gone, & sometimes wanted
To slip in a reminder, how Mary Lou
Williams' "Polka Dots & Moonbeams"
Never made the swelling go down.
His carpenter's apron always bulged
With old nails, a claw hammer
Looped at his side & extension cords
Coiled around his feet.
Words rolled from under the pressure
Of my ballpoint: Love,
Baby, Honey, Please.
We sat in the quiet brutality
Of voltage meters & pipe threaders,
Lost between sentences . . .
The gleam of a five-pound wedge
On the concrete floor
Pulled a sunset
Through the doorway of his toolshed.
I wondered if she laughed
& held them over a gas burner.
My father could only sign
His name, but he'd look at blueprints
& say how many bricks

Formed each wall. This man,
Who stole roses & hyacinth
For his yard, would stand there
With eyes closed & fists balled,
Laboring over a simple word, almost
Redeemed by what he tried to say.

Salomé

I had seen her
Before, nearly hidden
Behind those fiery branches
As she dove nude
Into the creek.
This white girl
Who moved with ease
On her side of the world
As if she were the only
Living thing. Her breasts
Rose like swamp orchids
On the water's rhythm
Along an old path –
Suckholes & whirlpools
Reaching down for years.
A hundred yards away
The black baptists
From Tree of Life
& Sweet Beulah
Dunked white-robed boys & girls.
The fishing cork danced
& then disappeared, but I couldn't
Move in my tall greenness.
A water snake crawled
Along the stunted oak
That grew half in water,
Half in earth. I knew
Salomé's brother, Cleanth,
Hung our cat with a boot lace
From a crooked fencepost –

Knew he pulled on the cat's
Hind legs, a smile on his face,
& it wouldn't be long before
He would join her in the creek
& they'd hold each other
Like Siamese twins at the State Fair,
Swimmers trapped under
A tyranny of roots, born
With one heart.

Slam, Dunk, & Hook

Fast breaks. Lay ups. With Mercury's
Insignia on our sneakers,
We outmaneuvered to footwork
Of bad angels. Nothing but a hot
Swish of strings like silk
Ten feet out. In the roundhouse
Labyrinth our bodies
Created, we could almost
Last forever, poised in midair
Like storybook sea monsters.
A high note hung there
A long second. Off
The rim. We'd corkscrew
Up & dunk balls that exploded
The skullcap of hope & good
Intention. Lanky, all hands
& feet . . . sprung rhythm.
We were metaphysical when girls
Cheered on the sidelines.
Tangled up in a falling,
Muscles were a bright motor
Double-flashing to the metal hoop
Nailed to our oak.
When Sonny Boy's mama died
He played nonstop all day, so hard
Our backboard splintered.
Glistening with sweat,
We rolled the ball off
Our fingertips. Trouble
Was there slapping a blackjack

Against an open palm.
Dribble, drive to the inside,
& glide like a sparrow hawk.
Lay ups. Fast breaks.
We had moves we didn't know
We had. Our bodies spun
On swivels of bone & faith,
Through a lyric slipknot
Of joy, & we knew we were
Beautiful & dangerous.

Work

I won't look at her.
My body's been one
Solid motion from sunrise,
Leaning into the lawnmower's
Roar through pine needles
& crabgrass. Tiger-colored
Bumblebees nudge pale blossoms
Till they sway like silent bells
Calling. But I won't look.
Her husband's outside Oxford,
Mississippi, bidding on miles
Of timber. I wonder if he's buying
Faulkner's ghost, if he might run
Into Colonel Sartoris
Along some dusty road.
Their teenage daughter & son sped off
An hour ago in a red Corvette
For the tennis courts,
& the cook, Roberta,
Only works a half day
Saturdays. This antebellum house
Looms behind oak & pine
Like a secret, as quail
Flash through branches.
I won't look at her. Nude
On a hammock among elephant ears
& ferns, a pitcher of lemonade
Sweating like our skin.
Afternoon burns on the pool
Till everything's blue,

Till I hear Johnny Mathis
Beside her like a whisper.
I work all the quick hooks
Of light, the same unbroken
Rhythm my father taught me
Years ago: *Always give
A man a good day's labor*.
I won't look. The engine
Pulls me like a dare.
Scent of honeysuckle
Sings black sap through mystery,
Taboo, law, creed, what kills
A fire that is its own heart
Burning open the mouth.
But I won't look
At the insinuation of buds
Tipped with cinnabar.
I'm here, as if I never left,
Stopped in this garden,
Drawn to some Lotus-eater. Pollen
Explodes, but I only smell
Gasoline & oil on my hands,
& can't say why there's this bed
Of crushed narcissus
As if gods wrestled here.

Songs for My Father

I told my brothers I heard
You & mother making love,
Your low moan like blues
Bringing them into the world.
I didn't know if you were laughing
Or crying. I held each one down
& whispered your song in their ears.
Sometimes I think they're still jealous
Of our closeness, having forgotten
We had to square off & face each other,
My fists balled & cocked by haymakers.
That spring I lifted as many crossties
As you. They can't believe I can
Remember when you had a boy's voice.

*

You were a quiet man
Who'd laugh like a hyena
On a hill, with your head
Thrown back, gazing up at the sky.
But most times you just worked
Hard, rooted in the day's anger
Till you'd explode. We always
Walked circles around
You, wider each year,
Hungering for stories
To save us from ourselves.
Like a wife who isn't touched,
We had to do something bad
Before you'd look into our eyes.

*

We spent the night before Easter
Coloring eggs & piling them into pyramids
In two crystal punch bowls.
Our suits, ties, white shirts, shoes,
All lined up for the next day.
We had memorized our passages
From the Bible, about the tomb
& the angel rolling back the stone.
You were up before daybreak,
In the sagebrush, out among goldenrod
& mustard weed, hiding the eggs
In gopher holes & underneath roots.
Mother always argued with you,
Wondering why you made everything so hard.

*

We stood on a wooden platform
Facing each other with sledgehammers,
A copper-tipped sieve sunken into the ground
Like a spear, as we threaded on five foot
Of galvanized pipe for the pump.
As if tuned to some internal drum,
We hammered the block of oak
Placed on top of the pipe.
It began inching downward
As we traded blows – one for you,
One for me. After a half hour
We threaded on another five foot. The sweat
Gleamed on our shirtless bodies, father
& son tied to each other until we hit water.

*

Goddamn you. Goddamn you.
If you hit her again I'll sail through
That house like a dustdevil.
Everyone & everything here
Is turning against you,
That's why I had to tie the dog
To a tree before you could chastise us.
He darted like lightning through the screen door.
I know you'll try to kill me
When it happens. You know
I'm your son & it's bound to happen.
Sometimes I close my eyes till I am
On a sea of falling dogwood blossoms,
But someday this won't work.

*

I confess, I am the ringleader
Who sneaked planks out of the toolshed,
Sawed & hammered together the wagon.
But I wasn't fool enough to believe
That you would've loved our work.
So, my brothers & I dug a grave
In the corner of the field for our wagon
That ran smooth as a Nat King Cole
Love ballad. We'd pull it around
The edge of our world & rebury it
Before the 5 o'clock mill whistle blew.
I bet it's still there, the wood gray
& light as the ribs of my dog Red
After somebody gunned him down one night.

*

You banged a crooked nail
Into a pine slab,

Wanting me to believe
I shouldn't have been born
With hands & feet
If I didn't do
Your kind of work.
You hated my books.
Sometimes at dusk,
I faced you like that
Childhood friend you trained
Your heart to always run
Against, the horizon crimson
As the eyes of a fighting cock.

*

I never asked you how you
Passed the driver's test,
Since you could only write
& read your name. But hell,
You were good with numbers;
Always counting your loot.
That Chevy truck swerved
Along back roads night & day.
I watched you use wire
& sunlight to train
The strongest limbs,
How your tongue never obeyed
The foreman, how the truck motor
Was stunted, frozen at sixty.

*

You wanted to fight
When I told you that a woman
Can get rid of a man
With a flake of lye

In his bread each day.
When you told her what I said
I bet the two of you made love
Till the thought flew out of your head.
Now, when you stand wax-faced
At the door, your eyes begging
Questions as you mouth wordless
Songs like a red-belly perch,
Assaying the scene for what it is,
I doubt if love can part my lips.

*

Sometimes you could be
That man on a red bicycle,
With me on the handlebars,
Just rolling along a country road
On the edge of July, honeysuckle
Lit with mosquito hawks.
We rode from under the shady
Overhang, back into sunlight.
The day bounced off car hoods
As the heat & stinking exhaust
Brushed against us like a dragon's
Roar, nudging the bike with a tremor,
But you steered us through the flowering
Dogwood like a thread of blood.

*

You lean on a yard rake
As dry leaves & grass smolder
In a ditch in mid March,
Two weeks before your sixty-first
Birthday. You say I look happy.
I must be in love. It is 1986,

Five months before your death.
You toss a stone at the two dogs
Hooked together in a corner of the yard.
You smile, look into my eyes
& say you want me to write you a poem.
I stammer for words. You
Toss another stone at the dogs
& resume raking the leafless grass.

*

I never said thanks for Butch,
The wooden dog you pulled by a string.
It was ugly as a baldheaded doll.
Patched with wire & carpenter's glue, something
I didn't believe you had ever loved.
I am sorry for breaking it in half.
I never meant to make you go
Stand under the falling snowflakes
With your head bowed on Christmas
Day. I couldn't look at Butch
& see that your grandmother Julia,
That old slave woman who beat you
As if that's all she knew, had put love
Into it when she carved the dog from oak.

*

I am unlike Kikuji
In Kawabata's *Thousand Cranes*,
Since I sought out one of your lovers
Before you were dead.
Though years had passed
& you were with someone else,
She thought I reminded her
Of a man she'd once known.

She pocketed the three dollars.
A big red lampshade bloodied
The room, as if held by a mad
Diogenes. Yes, she cried out,
But she didn't sing your name
When I planted myself in her.

*

You spoke with your eyes
Last time I saw you, cramped
Between a new wife & a wall. You couldn't
Recognize funeral dirt stamped down
With dancesteps. Your name & features half
X-ed out. I could see your sex,
Your shame, a gold-toothed pout,
As you made plans for the next house you'd build,
Determined to prove me wrong. I never knew
We looked so much like each other. Before
I could say I loved you, you began talking money,
Teasing your will with a cure in Mexico.
You were skinny, bony, but strong enough to try
Swaggering through that celestial door.

Memory Cave

A tallow worked into a knot
of rawhide, with a ball of waxy light
tied to a stick, the boy
scooted through a secret mouth
of the cave, pulled by the flambeau
in his hand. He could see
the gaze of agate eyes
& wished for the forbidden
plains of bison & wolf, years
from the fermented honey
& musty air. In the dried
slag of bear & bat guano,
the initiate stood with sleeping
gods at his feet, lost
in the great cloud of their one
breath. Their muzzles craved
touch. How did they learn
to close eyes, to see into
the future? Before the Before:
mammon was unnamed & mist
hugged ravines & hillocks.
The elders would test him
beyond doubt & blood. Mica
lit the false skies where
stalactite dripped perfection
into granite. He fingered
icons sunlight & anatase
never touched. Ibex carved
on a throwing stick, reindeer
worried into an ivory amulet,

& a bear's head. Outside,
the men waited two days
for him, with condor & bovid,
& not in a thousand years
would he have dreamt a woman
standing here beside a man,
saying, "This is as good
as the stag at Salon Noir
& the polka-dotted horses."
The man scribbles *Leo loves
Angela* below the boy's last bear
drawn with manganese dioxide
& animal fat. This is where
sunrise opened a door in stone
when he was summoned to drink
honey wine & embrace a woman
beneath a five-pointed star.
Lying there beside the gods
hefty & silent as boulders,
he could almost remember
before he was born, could see
the cliff from which he'd fall.

Out There There Be Dragons

Beyond King Ptolemy's dream
outside the broken
girdle of chance, beyond
the Lighthouse of Pharos
in a kingdom of sea turtles,
nothing can inter or outrun
a stormy heart. Beyond galleon
& disappearing lovers, a flame
flounces behind a glass crab
to signal a craggy reef
in the Bay of Alexandria.
Beyond archipelagos of drizzle
& salt, Armageddon & hellfire,
bearded seals turn into Helen's
mermaids sunning on a white beach
beside Paris, where blotches of ink
map omens. Beyond Atlantis
uncovered by desert winds
phantom armies ride against,
necklace of shark teeth
adorn virgins. When earth
dilates, the known magnifies
till unknowns tincture silk,
till pomegranates bleed
redemption into soil.
Sirens cry across dark
waters, as anguelle becomes air,
beyond the mapmaker's omphalos
where hydra first mounted Venus.

The Song Thief

      Up there
in that diorama of morning
light through springtime branches,
how many feathered lifetimes
sifted down through green
leaves, how many wars sprung up
& ended before the cowbird figured out
laws of gravity in Cloudcuckooland,
before the songbird's egg
was nudged from its nest?
Maybe a flock followed a herd
of heifers across a pasture,
pecking wildflower seed
from fresh dung
when the first urge of switcheroo
flashed in their dirt-colored heads.
What nature of creature comforts
taught the unsung cells this art,
this shell game of odds
& percentages in the serpent's leafy
Babylon? Only the cowbird's mating song
fills the air until their young
are ravenous as five
of the seven deadly sins
woven into one.

Ode to a Drum

Gazelle, I killed you
for your skin's exquisite
touch, for how easy it is
to be nailed to a board
weathered raw as white
butcher paper. Last night
I heard my daughter praying
for the meat here at my feet.
You know it wasn't anger
that made me stop my heart
till the hammer fell. Weeks
ago, I broke you as a woman
once shattered me into a song
beneath her weight, before
you slouched into that
grassy hush. But now
I'm tightening lashes,
shaping hide as if around
a ribcage, stretched
like five bowstrings.
Ghosts cannot slip back
inside the body's drum.
You've been seasoned
by wind, dust & sunlight.
Pressure can make everything
whole again, brass nails
tacked into the ebony wood
your face has been carved
five times. I had to drive
trouble from the valley.

Trouble in the hills.
Trouble on the river
too. There's no kola nut,
palm wine, fish, salt,
or calabash. Kadoom.
Kadoom. Kadooom. Ka-
doooom. Kadoom. Now
I have beaten a song back into you,
rise & walk away like a panther.

Eclogue at Daybreak

His unlidded eyes a wish
always coming true,
as his body slithered
from a sheath of skin
half-alive on the grass
like a final lesson on escape.
He moved only when other things
strayed beyond suspicion.
The worlds inside sleep
couldn't hold him. In an arcade
somewhere in a marketplace
he was Houdini reincarnated
in a box. Soon came the hour
he was created for: a woman,
free-footed as Isadora
in sashes, draped his body
over hers. An apprentice
placed an apple in her left hand
& lush gardens sprouted across
three canvases. Her smooth skin,
how his wedge-shaped head
lingered between her breasts,
left him drowsy. The clocks
sped up. A cruel season
fell across their pose
as they began a slow dance.
She reshaped the pattern of skulls
on his yellow skin, a deep
falling inside him when her hips
quivered & arms undulated,
stealing the pleas of prey.

Confluence

I've been here before, dreaming myself
backwards, among grappling hooks of light.

True to the seasons, I've lived every word
spoken. Did I walk into someone's nightmare?

Hunger quivers on a fleshly string
at the crossroad. So deep is the lore,

there's only tomorrow today where darkness
splinters & wounds the bird of paradise.

On paths that plunge into primordial
green, Echo's laughter finds us together.

In the sweatshops of desire men think
if they don't die the moon won't rise.

All the dead-end streets run into one
moment of bliss & sleight of hand.

Beside the Euphrates, past the Tigris,
up the Mississippi. Bloodline & clockwork.

The X drawn where we stand. Trains
follow rivers that curve around us.

The distant night opens like a pearl
fan, a skirt, a heart, a drop of salt.

When we embrace, we are not an island
beyond fables & the blue exhaust of commerce.

When the sounds of River Styx punish
trees, my effigy speaks to the night owl.

Our voices break open the pink magnolia
where struggle is home to the beast in us.

All the senses tuned for the Hawkesbury,
labyrinths turning into lowland fog.

Hand in hand, feeling good, we walk
phantoms from the floating machine.

When a drowning man calls out,
his voice follows him downstream.

Eclogue at Twilight

The three wrestle in the grass
five or ten minutes, shaking blooms
& winged seeds to the ground.
The lioness lays a heavy paw on the jackal's chest,
almost motherly. His mate
backs off a few yards. Eyeball
to eyeball, they face each other
before she bites into his belly
& tugs out the ropy entrails
like loops of wet gauze.
Time stops. She'd moved
through the tall yellow sage
as they copulated,
stood only a few feet
away, enveloped in the scent
that drew them together.
When they first saw her
there, they couldn't stop.
Is this how panic & cunning
seethe into the bloodstream?
Without the power to forgive,
locked in ritual, the fight
began before they uncoupled.
A vulture, out of the frame,
draws an unbroken spiral
against the plains & sky.
Black quills scribble
slow as the swing of a hypnotist's
gold chain. For a moment, it seems
she's snuggling up to the jackal.

Maybe the wild aroma of sex
plagues the yellow grass.
A drizzle adds its music
to the background,
& a chorus of young girls
chants from across the hills.
For a man who stumbles
on this scene, with Hegel
& awe in his head, he can't
say if his mouth is opened
by the same cry & song.

The Tally

They're counting nails,
barrels of salt pork,
sacks of tea & sugar,
links of hemp, bolts of cloth
with dead colors, the whole
shape & slack of windy sails
down to galley planks
& clapboard hued by shame.
They're raising & lowering
an anchor clustered with urchins,
wondering if sandstone
can be taught a lesson
if inscribed with names & proclamations.
Snuff, powdered wigs –
redcoats run hands over
porcelain & silverware.
They're uncrating hymnals,
lace, volumes of Hobbes,
Rousseau, & kegs of rum.
Rats scurry across the deck
down the wharf, & a gaggle
of guinea fowl calls to a lost sky
from a row of slatted boxes.
Knives & forks, wooden pegs,
balls of twine, vats of tallow,
& whet stones. They're counting women
& men: twenty-two prostitutes, ten
pickpockets, one forger, countless
thieves of duck eggs & black bread.
A soldier pries open a man's fists

to tally twelve marigold seeds –
here for lobbing off a half pound
of butter. Deck hands winch in
the drag of lines. A young officer
surveys the prettiest women, before
stashing *The Collected Quotations
of Pythagoras* for the governor.
Albatross perched on the mast
await another burial at sea,
shadowing a stoic nightingale
in a bamboo cage mended with yarn
where a red-headed woman kneels,
whispering his song to him.

Heroes of Waterloo

Here's the pub they conked
drunks over the head & shanghaied
them on carts rolled down shafts
to the quay. After schooners
of cider, I see the half-dazed
waking to sea monsters
outside The Heads.

Your hands anchor me to the antipodes
as "Stormy Monday Blues"
drowns the mermaid's lament,
& suddenly a man wants to bop
me over the head. The night
steals memories from sandstone
walls the convicts cut.

Larrikins shout middies of Strongbow
& point to the trapdoor
where Captain Hook hides
on the other side of jetlag.
But with your fingertips
at the nape, the blood's sextant,
I can't move beyond the body's true north.

In the Mirror

Joey, you're behind shades
borrowed from Teach on page 67
of *The Australian Woman's Mirror*
March 29, 1961. Under the canopy

of a wide hat, with notebook & pencil,
you gaze out across the Kimberleys,
one step from the corner of time
crawling from a rainbow serpent's cave.

Less than the Crown of Thorns
along the Great Barrier Reef,
I look to see if a crack's started
in the black porcelain of your face.

No, I haven't swum the Fitzroy
near the Liveringa Sheep Station
or felt as small as you, Joey,
under the bigness of your sky,

but I hope you've outlasted
pages I found in the Opportunity Shop
where silver moths began years ago
to eat away your name.

Messages

They brand themselves with hearts
& dragons, *omni vincit amor*
wreathing the handles of daggers,
skulls with flowers between teeth,
& dotted lines across throats
saying *c-u-t-a-l-o-n-g-h-e-r-e*.
Epigraphs chiseled into marble
glisten with sweat.
Madonna quivers on a bicep
as fingers dance over a pinball machine.
Women pose with x's drawn through names
to harden features & bring knifethrowers
into their lives. A stripper in the neon
doorway of The Pink Pussycat
shows how the tattoo artist's hands
shook, as if the rose
were traced on her skin
with carbon paper & colored-in by bad luck . . .
red as a lost cartographer's ink.
A signature under her left nipple.

Bennelong's Blues

You're here again, old friend.
You strut around like a ragtag redcoat
bellhop, glance up for a shooting star
& its woe, & wander in & out the cove
you rendezvoused with Governor Phillip
after Wil-le-me-ring speared him beside a beached
whale. We've known each other for years.
You're unchanged. But me, old scapegoat,
I never knew I was so damn happy
when we first met. Each memory
returns like heartbreak's boomerang.
You didn't tell me you were a scout,
a bone pointer, a spy,
someone to stand between new faces
& gods. I didn't know your other four
ceremonial names, hero in clownish clothes,
till another dead man whispered into my ear.

Quatrains for Ishi

When they swoop on you hobbled there
almost naked, encircled by barking dogs
at daybreak beside a slaughterhouse
in Oroville, outside Paradise,

California, draped in a canvas scrap
matted with dung & grass seed,
slack-jawed men aim rifles
at your groin. *Wild Man*

hums through telegraph wires,
as women from miles around
try to tame your tongue
by cooking family recipes

& bringing bowls of ambrosia
to the jail. Hungry & sick,
lonely & scared, you never touch
the food. Not even the half-breeds

can open your mouth with Wintu,
Spanish, & Maidu. Days pass
till an anthropologist faces you
with his list of lost words,

rolling them off his tongue
like beads of old honey. But you
are elsewhere, covering your head
with a mourning cap of pine pitch,

in earshot of Wild Horse Corral,
as winds steal prayers of the dead
from Kingsley Cave. It takes
more than years of moonlight

to torch bones down to ashes
to store in a rock cairn
at Mill Creek. You are there,
Ishi, with the last five men

strong enough to bend bows,
with the last twelve voices
of your tribe. When you hear
the anthropologist say *siwini*,

the two of you dance
& bang your hands against
the wooden cot, running fingers
along the grain of yellow pine.

On Main Street, where gold
fever left the air years ago,
you're now The Wild Man of Oroville
beside a new friend. When the train

whistles, you step behind a cottonwood
shading the platform, afraid of The Demon
your mother forbade you to venture near.
What is it, does a voice call to you

out of windy chapparal,
out of Wowunupo mu terna,
to urge you back? Down
that rainbow of metal light

& sparks – then ferried across
Carquinez Straits – to the Oakland Mole.
The Golden Gate frames water
meeting sky, as a trolley car

lumbers uphill to your new home
at the Museum of Anthropology.
Here, in this ancient dust
on artifacts pillaged from Egypt

& Peru, I know why a man like you
laughs with one hand over his mouth.
Also, I know if I think of you
as me, you'll disappear. Ishi,

you're like a Don Juan
sitting beside Mrs. Gifford
calling birds. Who's Miss Fannie
in this photo from St. Louis?

Friend, what can you say
about these stone charms
from Lone Pine & England,
& are you still going to Chico

for that *Fiesta Arborea*?
How about this Sierra Club
walk from Buena Vista Park?
Here's another sack of acorns,

a few bundles of buckeye, hazel
shoots & alder. There's a sadness
in these willow branches, but no mock
orange. Pine needles have taught me

humility, & I'll never string
a bow or chip a blade from a block
of obsidian. The salmon harpoon
glides through the air as if

your mind entered the toggles
& shaft. I walk backwards
into Bear's Hiding Place
like you showed me – coming when

gone, on the other side of the river
standing here beside you, a snare
of milkweed coiled on the ground
like a curse inside a dream.

Back in your world of leaves,
you journey ten thousand miles
in a circle, hunted for years
inside the heart, till you wake

talking to a shadow in a robe
of wildcat pelts. Here
the day's bright as the purse
you carry your sacred tobacco in.

Your lungs are like thumbprints
on a negative, with you at a hospital
window as workmen walk girders:
All a same monkey-tee. I know why

a man doesn't sleep with the moon
in his face, how butter steals
the singing voice, & how a frog
cures a snakebite. At the museum

in your counting room, we gaze
down at the divided garden, past
bearded phantoms on streetcorners
perfumed with incense & herbs,

signaling the hills closer
where eucalyptus stores up oils
for a new inferno in the Sutro
Forest. Here's your five hundred

& twenty half dollars
saved in thirteen film cases –
your unwound watch now ticks
as the pot of glue hardens

among your arrows & knots
of deer sinews. March 25
at noon is as good a time to die
as to be born. A bluish sun

conspires to ignite the pyre
of bone awls & pendants of Olivella
shells, as a bear stands in Deer Creek
waving a salmon at the sky.

for Luzma

Nude Interrogation

Did you kill anyone over there? Angelica shifts her gaze from the Janis Joplin poster to the Jimi Hendrix, lifting the pale muslin blouse over her head. The blacklight deepens the blues when the needle drops into the first groove of "All Along the Watch-tower." I don't want to look at the floor. *Did you kill anyone? Did you dig a hole, crawl inside, and wait for your target?* Her miniskirt drops into a rainbow at her feet. Sandalwood incense hangs a slow comet of perfume over the room. I shake my head. She unhooks her bra and flings it against a bookcase made of plywood and cinderblocks. *Did you use an M-16, a hand-grenade, a bayonet, or your own two strong hands, both thumbs pressed against that little bird in the throat?* She stands with her left thumb hooked into the elastic of her sky-blue panties. When she flicks off the blacklight, snowy hills rush up to the windows. *Did you kill anyone over there? Are you right-handed or left-handed? Did you drop your gun afterwards? Did you kneel beside the corpse and turn it over?* She's nude against the falling snow. *Yes.* The record spins like a bull's eye on the far wall of Xanadu. *Yes,* I say. *I was scared of the silence. The night was too big. And afterwards, I couldn't stop looking up at the sky.*

The Poplars

Half in Monet's colors, headlong into this light, like someone lost along Daedalus' footpath winding back into the brain, hardly here. Doubts swarm like birds around a scarecrow – straw pulled from underneath a work cap.

Church bells alloy the midwest sky. How many troubled feet walked this path smooth? Is it safe to go back to Chu Lai? She's brought me halfway home again, away from the head floating down into my out-stretched hands.

I step off the path, sinking into one-hundred-years of leaves. Like trapped deer, we face each other. Her hands in his. His blue eyes. Her Vietnamese face. Am I a ghost dreaming myself back to flesh?

I stand in the skin's prison. A bluejay squawks till its ragged song pulls me out into the day burning like a vaporous temple of joss sticks. June roses in beds of mulch and peat moss surround me. I hear her nervous laughter at my back, among the poplars.

I can't hear my footsteps. I stop, turn and gaze at the lovers against an insistent green like stained glass. I walk toward a car parked near the church. Birds sing and flit in the raucous light. I hear the car's automatic locks click, sliding like bullets into the chamber of a gun.

On Third Street, the morning's alive with coeds hurrying into the clangor of bells, Saturday night asleep beneath their skin. Flowers herd them toward Jesus – cutworms on the leaves, at the roots.

Surgery

Every spring, sure as the dogwood's clockwork, someone hacksaws off Odysseus' penis. And it lies dumbly at his feet, a door-knocker to a limestone castle, the fountain spraying out a Medusa halo. In this watery mist, with a contrary sunlight glinting the bronze, there's only an outline of Eumaeus handing a quiver of arrows and a bow to him. Rivulets of water make the penis tremble, as if it were the final, half-alive offering to the gods.

Fifty yards past the fountain, on the other side of the quad, I step among lotus-eaters sunning in each other's arms. Mockingbirds and jays squabble overhead, dive-bombing Dutch elms. This unholy racket doesn't faze sunbathers and tree surgeons. As if they're fathering their destruction, branches fall into a pile, and the workmen pack beetle-eaten crevices with a white medicine, something like mortar – whiter than flesh.

I stop beneath an elm and clutch a half-dead branch. Momentarily, there's an old silence thick as memory. Claymores pop. Rifles and mortars answer, and then that silence again, as the slow light of tripflares drifts like a thousand falling handkerchiefs, lighting the concertina with arms and legs of sappers. Flares tied to little parachutes like magnolia blooming in the wounded air.

The sunbathers retreat into their abodes and the workmen feed the last branches into a big orange machine. The fountain's drained, and a man kneels before Odysseus. He holds the penis in one hand and a soldering torch in the other, his face hidden behind a black hood, beading a silver seam perfect enough to mend anyone's dream.

A Summer Night in Hanoi

When the moviehouse lights click off and images flicker-dance against the white walls, I hear Billie's whispered lament. *Hoi Chi Minh: The Man* rolls across the skin of five lynched black men, branding them with ideographic characters.

This scene printed on his eyelids is the one I was born with. My face is up there among the poplar leaves veined into stained glass. I'm not myself here, craving a mask of silk elusive as his four aliases.

He retouches photographs, paints antiques, gardens, cooks pastries, and loves and hates everything French. On his way to Chung-king to talk with Chiang K'ai-shek about fighting the Japanese, as day runs into night, he's arrested and jailed for fourteen months. Sitting here in the prison of my skin, I feel his words grow through my fingertips till I see his southern skies and old friends where mountains are clouds. As he tosses kernels of corn to carp, they mouth silent O's through the water.

Each face hangs like swollen breadfruit, clinging to jade leaves. How many eyes are on me, clustered in the hum of this dark theatre? The film flashes like heat lightning across a southern night, and the bloated orbs break open. Golden carp collage the five faces. The earth swings on a bellrope, limp as a body bag tied to a limb, and the moon overflows with blood.

A Reed Boat

The boat's tarred and shellacked to a water-repellent finish, just sway-dancing with the current's ebb, light as a woman in love. It pushes off again, cutting through lotus blossoms, sediment, guilt, unforgivable darkness. Anything with half a root or heart could grow in this lagoon.

There's a pull against what's hidden from day, all that hurts. At dawn the gatherer's shadow backstrokes across water, an instrument tuned for gods and monsters in the murky kingdom below. Blossoms lean into his fast hands, as if snapping themselves in half, giving in to some law.

Slow, rhetorical light cuts between night and day, like nude bathers embracing. The boat nudges deeper, with the ease of silverfish. I know by his fluid movements, there isn't the shadow of a bomber on the water anymore, gliding like a dream of death. Mystery grows out of the decay of dead things – each blossom a kiss from the unknown.

When I stand on the steps of Hanoi's West Lake Guest House, feeling that I am watched as I gaze at the boatman, it's hard to act like we're the only two left in the world. He balances on his boat of Ra, turning left and right, reaching through and beyond, as if the day is a woman he can pull into his arms.

The Hanoi Market

It smells of sea and earth, of things dying and newly born. Duck eggs, pig feet, mandarin oranges. Wooden bins and metal boxes of nails, screws, ratchets, balled copper wire, brass fittings, jet and helicopter gadgets, lug wrenches, bolts of silk, see-through paper, bamboo calligraphy pens, and curios hammered out of artillery shells.

Faces painted on coconuts. Polished to a knife-edge or sealed in layers of dust and grease, cogs and flywheels await secret missions. Aphrodisiacs for dream merchants. A silent storm moves through this place. Someone's worked sweat into the sweet loaves lined up like coffins on a stone slab.

She tosses her blonde hair back and smiles down at everyone. Is it the squid and shrimp we ate at lunch, am I seeing things? An adjacent stall blooms with peacock feathers. The T-shirt wavers like a pennant as a sluggish fan slices the humidity.

I remember her white dress billowing up in a blast of warm air from a steel grate in New York City, reminding me of Miss Firecracker flapping like a flag from an APC antenna. Did we kill each other for this?

I stop at a table of figurines. What was meant to tear off a leg or arm twenty years ago, now is a child's toy I can't stop touching.

Maybe Marilyn thought she'd erase herself from our minds, but she's here when the fan flutters the T-shirt silkscreened with her face. The artist used five shades of red to get her smile right.

A door left ajar by a wedge of sunlight. Below the T-shirt, at the end of two rows of wooden bins, a chicken is tied directly across from a caged snake. Bright skin – deadly bite. I move from the chicken to the snake, caught in their hypnotic plea.

The Deck

I have almost nailed my left thumb to the 2 × 4 brace that holds the deck together. This Saturday morning in June, I have sawed 2 × 6s, T-squared and levelled everything with three bubbles sealed in green glass, and now the sweat on my tongue tastes like what I am. I know I'm alone, using leverage to swing the long boards into place, but at times it seems as if there are two of us working side by side like old lovers guessing each other's moves.

This hammer is the only thing I own of yours, and it makes me feel I have carpentered for years. Even the crooked nails are going in straight. The handsaw glides through grease. The toenailed stubs hold. The deck has risen up around me, and now it's strong enough to support my weight, to not sway with this old, silly, wrong-footed dance I'm about to throw my whole body into.

Plumbed from sky to ground, this morning's work can take nearly anything! With so much uproar and punishment, footwork and euphoria, I'm almost happy this Saturday.

I walk back inside and here you are. Plain and simple as the sunlight on the tools outside. Daddy, if you'd come back a week ago, or day before yesterday, I would have been ready to sit down and have a long talk with you. There were things I wanted to say. So many questions I wanted to ask, but now they've been answered with as much salt and truth as we can expect from the living.

Blessing the Animals

Two by two, past
the portals of paradise,
camels & pythons parade.
As if on best behavior,
civil as robed billy goats
& Big Bird, they stroll
down aisles of polished stone
at the Feast of St. Francis.
An elephant daydreams, nudging
ancestral bones down a rocky path,
but won't venture near the boy
with a white mouse peeking
from his coat pocket. Beyond
monkeyshine, their bellows
& cries are like prayers
to unknown planets & zodiac
signs. The ferret & mongoose
on leashes, move as if they know
things with a sixth sense.
Priests twirl hoops of myrrh.
An Australian blue cattle dog
paces a heaven of memories –
a butterfly on a horse's ear
bright as a poppy outside
Urbino. As if crouched
between good & bad, St. John
the Divine grows in quintessence
& limestone, & a hoorah of Miltonic
light falls upon alley rats
awaiting nighttime. Brother

ass, brother sparrowhawk,
& brother dragon. Two
by two, washed & brushed down
by love & human pride,
these beasts of burden
know they're the first
scapegoats. After sacred
oils & holy water, we huddle
this side of their knowing
glances, & they pass through
our lives, still loyal to thorns.

The Thorn Merchant's Daughter

When she cocks her head
the last carrier pigeon's ghost
cries out across a cobalt sky.
The glossy snapshot of her
draped in a sun-blanched dress
before a garden of stone phalluses
slants crooked in its gold frame.
She looks as if she's tiptoed
out of *Innocence Choosing Love
over Wealth*. A Janus-headed
figure tarries at a junction
with twelve versions of hell
& heaven. She's transfixed
by bluejays pecking dewy figs
down to the meaty promise of a heart.
She's *Mary Magdalen in the Grotto*,
& was eyeing Lee Morgan at Slugs'
when the pistol flash burned
through his solo. Her aliases
narrate tales from Nepal & Paris,
Texas, from Bathsheba to the woman
flaming like poppies against sky
at the theatre with John
Dillinger. To see her
straight, there's no choice
but to walk with a limp.

The Monkey House

He pressed his face against the bars,
watching the biggest male macaque
mount a statuesque female.
She gazed at the cage floor
& he looked up past
rafters of leaves & fiberglass,
squinting toward a sundial.
They were rocking back & forth,
grunting a chorus of muffled laughs.
A father covered his daughter's eyes
with both hands, but let his two sons look.
An old woman kept tugging
her husband's sleeve
as he stood munching Cracker
Jacks, searching for the toy
pistol or spinning top
at the bottom of the box.
He watched, stroking his beard,
a hundred yards away from the crowd
eating noontime sandwiches & sipping
thermoses of coffee. Joggers worked
the air with arms & legs,
& it seemed to him the monkeys
were making love to the rhythms
of the city. Also, he still can't
say why, but he was running
the term *ethnic cleansing* over
& over in his mind, like a stone
polishing itself in a box of sand.
There were tears in his eyes,

& he felt like he'd returned
to the scene of a crime.
When their bodies began to tremble
down to a split second, the other
monkeys began to slap the male
& beat his head like a drum.
Then, lost among the absurd
clocks, he turned to watch
leaves as they began to fall.

Dolphy's Aviary

We watched Baghdad's skyline
ignite, arms & legs entwined
as white phosphorus washed over
our bedroom, the sounds of war
turned down to a sigh. It was one
of those nights we couldn't let go
of each other, a midwestern storm
pressing panes till they trembled
in their sashes. Eric Dolphy
scored the firmament splitting
to bedrock, as the wind spoke
tongues we tried to answer.
At first, we were inside
muted chords, inside an orgasm
of secrets, & then cried out,
"Are those birds?" Midnight
streetlights yellowed the snow –
a fleeting ghost battalion
cremated in the bony cages
of tanks in sand dunes. Dolphy said
"Birds have notes between our notes . . ."
I could see them among oak rafters
& beams, beyond the burning cold,
melodious in cobweb & soot.
Like false angels up there
in a war of electrical wires
& bat skeletons caked with excrement,
we in winding sheets of desire
as their unbearable songs
startled us down.

Woebegone

We pierce tongue
& eyebrow, foreskin
& nipple, as if threading wishes
on gutstring. Gold bead
& question mark hook
into loopholes & slip
through. We kiss
like tiny branding irons.
Loved ones guard words
of praise, & demigods mortgage
nighttime. Beneath bruised
glamor, we say, "I'll show
how much I love you by
how many scars I wear."
As we steal the last
drops of anger, what can we
inherit from Clarksdale's blue
tenements? Medieval & modern,
one martyr strokes another
till Torquemada rises.
We trade bouquets
of lousewort, not for the red
blooms & loud perfume,
but for the lovely spikes.

Anodyne

I love how it swells
into a temple where it is
held prisoner, where the god
of blame resides. I love
slopes & peaks, the secret
paths that make me selfish.
I love my crooked feet
shaped by vanity & work
shoes made to outlast
belief. The hardness
coupling milk it can't
fashion. I love the lips,
salt & honeycomb on the tongue.
The hair holding off rain
& snow. The white moons
on my fingernails. I love
how everything begs
blood into song & prayer
inside an egg. A ghost
hums through my bones
like Pan's midnight flute
shaping internal laws
beside a troubled river.
I love this body
made to weather the storm
in the brain, raised
out of the deep smell
of fish & water hyacinth,
out of rapture & the first
regret. I love my big hands.

I love it clear down to the soft
quick motor of each breath,
the liver's ten kinds of desire
& the kidney's lust for sugar.
This skin, this sac of dung
& joy, this spleen floating
like a compass needle inside
nighttime, always divining
West Africa's dusty horizon.
I love the birthmark
posed like a fighting cock
on my right shoulder blade.
I love this body, this
solo & ragtime jubilee
behind the left nipple,
because I know I was born
to wear out at least
one hundred angels.

The Centaur

Shape-changer caught in the middle
Of rehearsal, here between beast
& man, like a young Chiron,
You pretend birthright,

Hoping Atalanta's arrow
Finds you on a lost path
In bloom. Yes, sometimes,
You can be loony as a drunken

Stunt man in Paradise, a bit
Of Theocritus's sad metaphysics
In your bones. One half tortures
The other for the romantic songs

Crooned at sunset. Unholy
Need & desire divide the season,
As you eat sugar from a nymph's palm,
Before she mounts & rides you into a man.

Ode to the Maggot

Brother of the blowfly
& godhead, you work magic
Over battlefields,
In slabs of bad pork

& flophouses. Yes, you
Go to the root of all things.
You are sound & mathematical.
Jesus Christ, you're merciless

With the truth. Ontological & lustrous,
You cast spells on beggars & kings
Behind the stone door of Caesar's tomb
Or split trench in a field of ragweed.

No decree or creed can outlaw you
As you take every living thing apart. Little
Master of earth, no one gets to heaven
Without going through you first.

Envy

Icarus imitated the golden plover,
Drawn toward a blue folly
Above, looping through echoes
Of a boy's prankish laughter,

Through an airy labyrinth
Of conjecture. A lifetime
Ahead of Daedalus, with noon sun
In his eyes, he outflew the bird's

Equilibrium, wondering how this
Small creature of doubt braved
The briny trade winds. Surely,
In a fanfare of uneclipsed wings

Driven by dash & breathless style,
He could outdo the plover's soars
& dares. But he couldn't stop
Counting feathers against salty sky.

Castrato

You've made me Little Red
Riding Hood. Mister Wolf
Has my scent on his breath,
& I've forgotten how to bluff

Shadows back into the hedgerow.
The same contralto is in my throat
Year after year. But the scalpel
Is what I remember most. Please note

This: hymns die on my tongue
Before they can heal.
Smooth as my sister's doll baby
Down there, I don't know how I feel

Or need. Entangled in so many
What-ifs. Neither north nor south.
I wish I knew how to stop women
From crying when I open my mouth.

Pan

Elizabeth, I must say,
Pan wasn't raising Cain among the reeds.
He had taken off his mask,
& was lying there, puffing ganja,

Blowing Rasta smoke rings
& nibbling on a golden mango,
When he glimpsed three naiads
Prancing beside the lily pond.

He rolled over & watched two ants
Struggle up a Sisyphean incline
With a moth. Silenus's brother
& father, scapegoat & earthly god,

He felt divided. The nymphs frolicked
As he played love & panic on his flute
Till Arcady drifted out of his head,
& then a whisper opened all the buds.

Lust

If only he could touch her,
Her name like an old wish
In the stopped weather of salt
On a snail. He longs to be

Words, juicy as passion fruit
On her tongue. He'd do anything,
Dance three days & nights
To make the most terrible gods

Rise out of ashes of the yew,
To step from the naked
Fray, to be as tender
As meat imagined off

The bluegill's pearlish
Bones. He longs to be
An orange, to feel fingernails
Run a seam through him.

Happenstance

Small things go wrong, line up
Like beads on a prayer necklace.
An abacus of desire, aces
On a slot machine in Gulfport,

& then a minor god finds himself
Speaking with Moloch's cocky tongue.
An airplane falls, a spaceship
Explodes in midair over paradise,

A nuclear meltdown sizzles
In the belly of a leaden calf,
& the Minotaur finds his way out
Of a classic loophole. Normal

Accident. Juice leaves a battery
& exiles us to primeval dark. Romeo
& Juliet divorce on TV, & dream aloud
Muscles they couldn't quite fit into love.

Gluttony

In a country of splendor & high
Ritual, in a fat land of zeros,
Sits a man with string & bone
For a stylus, hunched over his easel,

Captured by perfection.
But also afflictions live behind
Electric fences, among hedges
& a whirlwind of roses, down

To where he sits beside a gully
Pooling desires. He squints
Till the mechanical horizon is one
Shadow play against bruised sky,

Till the smoky perfume limps
Into undergrowth. He balls up
Another sheet in unblessed fingers, always
Ready to draw the thing that is all mouth.

A Famous Ghost

I thought happiness my birthright
& married the bone structure
In mother's dreams, his English
Impeccable. Though they sift

My ashes & swear I fought
The shadows of his lovers,
I am not Propertius's Cynthia.
Where I stand, it is still '63

& the flags are at half-mast.
I never wanted to be famous,
But couldn't lift my head off
The oven door. My last breath

Stole from his. Fumes slipped
Down like a prayer to the Cubist
In the basement. No, I'm not Hostia,
Though I unlaced a corset of stardust.

A Kind of Xenia

Did she linger in a wintry bed
Reading *Leaves of Grass*,
Stroking a pale breast
With a dreamy hand, half lost

In Whitman's operatic springtime
Of words, swept into estral hours
Like Giorgione's Venus, before
She rose to sit nude at an oak desk

& offer herself to this maestro?
Did the letter travel by horse,
Rail, by foot, for long days,
A week? A horned owl called

Night's prey in voluminous air
As her naked sighs miles away
Escaped when his fingers
Opened the fragrant paper.

Avarice

At six, she chewed off
The seven porcelain buttons
From her sister's christening gown
& hid them in a Prince Albert can

On a sill crisscrossing the house
In the spidery crawl space.
She'd weigh a peach in her hands
Till it rotted. At sixteen,

She gazed at her little brother's
June bugs pinned to a sheet of cork.
Assaying their glimmer, till she
Buried them beneath a fig tree's wide,

Green skirt. Now, twenty-six,
Locked in the beauty of her bones,
She counts eight engagement rings
At least twelve times each day.

Rollerblades

Knucklehead spins on a wish & lucky
Star, dividing the city into hellbent
Circles, one improvisation to the next
Double-or-nothing dare. He grabs the bumper

Of a Yellow Cab & traverses Central Park,
Skirring & looping through rings, plugged
Into the Delfonics & Beastie Boys.
Zip, skid, & bone spindle . . .

Knucklehead hangs inside the bottom half
Of Odysseus's dreamt map to a country
Of lotus-eaters, E-mail, & goof-off.
Hugging curves beside the thieves of his image,

He ducks into a labyrinth of close
Calls. Their eyes collide. Knucklehead
Pivots, as if the four wheels of each blade
Could guillotine an apparition's last effigy.

Meditations on a File

I weigh you, a minute in each hand,
With the sun & a woman's perfume
In my senses, a need to smooth
Everything down. You belong

To a dead man, made to fit
A keyhole of metal to search
For light, to rasp burrs off
In slivers thin as hair, true

Only to slanted grooves cut
Across your tempered spine.
I'd laugh when my father said
Rat-tail. Now, slim as hope

& solid as remorse
In your red mausoleum,
Whenever I touch you
I crave something hard.

The God of Land Mines

He sits on a royal purple cushion
Like a titanic egg. Dogs whimper
& drag themselves on all fours through dirt
When a breeze stirs his sweet perfume.

He looks like a legless, armless
Humpty-Dumpty, & if someone waves
A photo of an amputee outside the Imperial
Palace in Hue, he'd never blink.

When he thinks *doors*, they swing open.
When dust gushes on the horizon
His face is a mouthless smile.
He can't stop loving steel.

He's oblong & smooth as a watermelon.
The contracts arrive already signed.
Lately, he feels like seeds in a jar,
Swollen with something missing.

Postscript to a Summer Night

As if he'd stood too long facing
A pharaoh in the Temple of Karnak
Or Hermes of Siphnos, one night
J. R. Midas copied his penis

On the company's Xerox machine,
Lying across a bed of hot light.
He was thirty-three, still half
Invincible, & scribbled on each: *I am*

*On fire with love, & all the more fire
Because I am rejected* . . . He x-ed out
Galatea, & wrote in names of the two
New district managers: *Melissa, Amy*

Lou. He hung his coat & tie on a hook,
Then strolled down to the docks
& walked under an orange moon
Till his clothes turned to rags.

The God of Variables

He nudges me out of Shangri-La
Collaged with Victoria's Secret,
As he gazes down like Socrates,
Saying, *Now, suppose Nicole*

*Simpson weighed 300 pounds
Or if she'd been a Dorothy
Dandridge?* I shake my head
& his notes blur into Dow Jones.

*Okay. Now let's drift back
To Emmett Till, to a wolf
Whistle in a town called Money,
To a night swollen with bullfrogs*

& honeysuckle. A cotton-gin wheel
Spins on the Tallahatchie. He pokes me
With a blue finger. *Now, if Louise
Woodward was a descendant of Sancho—*

Anger

We can cut out Nemesis's tongue
By omission or simple analysis.
Doesn't this sin have to marry
Another, like a wishbone

Worked into meat, to grow
Deadly? Snared within
The blood's quick night,
Our old gods made of sex

& wit, of nitrate & titanium,
Hurl midnight thunderbolts
& lightning. Are we here
Because they must question

Every death in an alley,
Every meltdown? We know
We wouldn't be much, if thorns
Didn't drive light into wet blooms.

Crow Lingo

Can you be up to any good
Grouped into a shadow against Venus,
Congregated on power lines around
The edges of cornfields?

Luck. Curse. A wedding.
Death. I have seen you peck
Pomegranates & then cawcawcaw
Till hornets rise from purple flesh

& juice. I know you're plotting
An overthrow of the government
Of sparrows & jays, as the high council
Of golden orioles shiver among maple

& cottonwood. Your language
Of passwords has no songs,
No redemption in wet feathers
Slicked back, a crook's iridescent hair.

Euphony

Hands make love to thigh, breast, clavicle,
Willed to each other, to the keyboard –
Searching the whole forest of compromises
Till the soft engine kicks in, running

On honey. Dissonance worked
Into harmony, evenhanded
As Art Tatum's plea to the keys.
Like a woman & man who have lived

A long time together, they know how
To keep the song alive. Wordless
Epics into the cold night, keepers
Of the fire – the right hand lifts

Like the ghost of a sparrow
& the left uses every motionless muscle.
Notes divide, balancing each other,
Love & hate tattooed on the fingers.